Dear Tony Oursler —

I hope you find "Mother" references to your lovely Grace, agreeable. I did so enjoy working with her, and truly regretted Lou's restraint.

Good luck in your retirement — but keep your mind challenged — you have much yet to contribute —

Cordially,
Starr

Grace — see paper on Guideposts 164 through 178

"Hello God. Can We Talk?"

Starr West Jones

Library of Congress Cataloging-in-Publication Data

Jones, Starr West.
  Hello God, can we talk?

1. Spiritual life. 2. Jones, Starr West.
I. Title.
BL624.J65 1988   248.4   87-17672
ISBN 0-8119-0712-0

International Standard Book Number: 0–8119–0712–0
Library of Congress Catalog Card Number: 87–17672

For information address:

Frederick Fell Publishers, Inc.
2131 Hollywood Boulevard
Hollywood, Florida   33020

Published simultaneously in Canada by Book Center, Montreal, Canada

Manufactured in the United States of America
1 2 3 4 5 6 7 8 9 0

"Hello God. Can We Talk?"

Starr West Jones

To my beloved Ginny
and our
Quad Squad

Table of Contents

"Hello God. Can We Talk?"

"Hello God. Can We Talk?"

Credits Sheet
Cover photo, Lightning over Kitt Peak, © Gary Ladd.
Used by special permission.
Author's portrait photo, by Jack Ryer, Pawling, N.Y.

Introduction

Throughout my life I have talked with God, questioning, debating and on occasion wrestling with Him. I have experienced hunger, tragedy, challenging adventure and piercingly beautiful love in this magnificent world into which the Creator ordained that I be born. I don't feel that I have to be "born again" in order to know Him.

The need to satisfy spiritual hunger, as well as the physical hungers of the body, has been with me in overlapping patterns ever since I entered this world.

In the seventy-eight years that I have enjoyed the challenges of this beautiful, exquisitely complex globe which the Creator has placed in orbit in His limitless universe I have, through persistent questing, always been able to discover His presence wherever I sought spiritual nourishment. In retrospect, I now realize that my life has been one long, often intense, sometimes disjointed, conversation with God. I have sought Him in the great out-of-doors, in Moslem mosques, in Jewish synagogues and Buddhist temples, in every type of recognized—or splintered—church of Christian persuasion, in the bedlam of big city living, in the fury of battle, in the white silence of snow-covered mountain peaks—and He was always there.

Frequently these conversations have provided real satisfaction to my spiritual hunger. On other occasions they have served only to intensify, still further, that appetite. Often, too, these dialogues have become entangled with the parallel struggle to satisfy my basic body hungers, so closely do the spiritual and the physical overlap each other. Yet that, I feel certain, is what the Creator intended for both are vital to the development of the whole personality. Only when this is accomplished will such a person be enabled to bring fully alive the Divine spark of individuality which makes each of us utterly different from all other human beings. Only then is each of us able to add his or her unique contribution to making this world a better place for those who will follow. This, I have come to believe, is the ultimate purpose for which we are created.

What I am setting down on these pages is intended not to persuade others to my interpretation of that Divine purpose, but rather to share, from the actual experience of a long and somewhat complex life, views that I have seen from what some might call the window of my soul. By whatever process the insight was gained, I know that the perceptive ability was with me from the instant I was born into God's eternally evolving universe in this moment of eternity.

Hello, God. Can We Talk?

rateful acknowledgment is made for the special permission granted to the author to use extracts of copyrighted material as follows:

Lines from the Fifth act of Brian Hooker's version of Edmund Rostand's play, *Cyrano de Bergerac,* published and copyrighted in 1923 by Henry Holt Company. Used by permission of the Publisher.

Lines from the Fourth act of Eugene O'Neill's play *The Great God Brown,* published and copyrighted in 1932 by Liveright Inc. Used by permission of Random House, Inc., and also by Yale University (as trustees for the works of Eugene O'Neill) from their Collection of American Literature in the Beinecke Rare Book and Manuscript Library.

Extracts from articles by Joseph Stacey, Harry Golden and Mary Elizabeth Burke, as they appeared in the November 1973 issue of Arizona Highways magazine, are used by courtesy of Arizona Highways and by special permission of the authors, Joseph Stacey and Mary Elizabeth Burke; and as abridged from *Only In America* by Harry Golden (Thomas Y. Crowell Co.) copyrighted in 1958 by Harry Golden. Reprinted by permission of Harper & Row Publishers Inc.

Acknowledgment

Many years ago my wife had suggested that I should try to put down on paper, for the future enlightenment of our sons, the discoveries which I had made in my search for the meaning of life. But it was my good friend, Frederick Fell, who challenged me to put them into book form. And it was Fred, who for five years encouraged me, in my slow moments goaded me and whipped up my enthusiasm for the subject so that I dug deeper into the hidden recesses of my mind than I had ever intended to reach, to share with others. I am forever grateful to him—he has been more than a friend, more than my publisher; Fred Fell has been my literary mentor.

CHAPTER I

The Rectory Years:

The Shock That Started My Argument With The Creator

It was a cold morning, that 20th of January 1906, in the rectory of the small Episcopal church in Oskaloosa, Iowa, where I first saw the light of this planet. My parents knew then that I was born terribly hungry, for I chewed incessantly on my fist. As a matter of fact, my stomach seemed never satisfied and I lost weight rapidly, my skin was yellowish and I was so tiny I could have been cradled in a cigar box. My maternal grandmother, who was visiting us from California, told my deeply concerned mother, "Polly, don't fret yourself about that little banana. He won't live, but you'll have other children. You're young yet."

But my dear mother, a pretty brunette with deep, brilliant blue eyes, was inordinately talented in the literary arts and possessed of a magnificent will power. She wasn't about to give up on her first-born son, the second child of a marriage she had entered upon in order to escape what she considered a dreary life as a

1

teacher in a San Antonio private girl's school run by her maternal uncle. Thus, when the family doctor who delivered me had told mother that her milk flow was inadequate to meet the demands of my outsized appetite and recommended a wet nurse, my mother was indignant. Such a thought was repugnant to mother's ideal of true motherhood. "I'll make more milk!" she told him.

Mother turned to my father and told him, perhaps dramatically, for everything my mother did or said was always expressed as though it were a scene upon the stage. "John get me some beer. I've heard it increases the flow of a mother's milk. Get me some beer, today!" Whereupon my wonderfully kind and cheerful father, an Episcopal clergyman whose broad approach to ecclesiastical thought was 100 years ahead of his time, now, ignoring the small-minded gossip which he knew would spring up following his action, brought home a case of beer and placed it beneath mother's bed. Each day mother drank it. Her milk responded, and I started to grow.

Eventually I attained a height of six-feet-two with a vigorous body but a never completely satisfied stomach. No doubt this hiatus was due to the ever present struggle for food which dominated the lean years of the first quarter of my life. Looking back now, it seems that hunger for food took precedence over other physical needs—the basic hungers for warmth, shelter and sex, though their day would come.

In those early years my spiritual hunger was supposedly provided for in the manner of my upbringing. As the oldest son of a vigorously active clergyman, church attendance was not only mandatory it was multitudinous. Until I was sixteen years old, not less than two—often as many as five—Sunday services saw me moving about the church chancel as acolyte or choir boy. Thus, the theology and dogma of Protestant-Christianity made its subliminal impression on my mind, there to be eventually doubted, deliberated and dissected in sometimes turbulent internal debate between myself and God.

Complicating this background, because both my father and mother agreed that the curriculum and teaching of public school education was inferior to that obtained in the parochial schools of the Roman Catholic Church, my sister and I and our three younger brothers all attended grammar and high school classes in those institutions. From the patient, disciplined teaching of the nuns of several different religious orders (and in my own high school years the brothers and priests of the Carmelite order) we received such a firm grounding in English grammar, composition, arithmetic and Latin that our lives were enriched beyond the measure of our contemporaries.

And, contrary to popular belief, these dedicated religious persons never tried to convert us. I think perhaps it was the similarity of the Anglican and Roman Catholic creeds and the structure of the service (except that in those days theirs was read in Latin and ours in English) which proved a bond, rather than a division, to our mutual understanding. I remember having many friendly, often involved, discussions on theological matters with the nuns and brothers, all of which fed and whetted my spiritual appetite.

While in later years I attended and enjoyed the ministry of numerous other churches, somehow I was reluctant to commit myself to full acceptance of any particular creed. Though I did not realize it then, I was rebelling at the limitations of spiritual horizons imposed by the dogmatic boundaries of organized churches. This internal questioning grew more intense with the years, until my need to satisfy spiritual hunger became a continuous search for the purpose in God's creation of this world and a demand for an answer to "why did He place me here?"

The first intimation of this dissatisfaction must have come to me when I was about nine years old. Dad had a parish in downtown Omaha, but our rectory home was a new house out in the suburbs. I think it was loaned by a businessman of the congregation who was anxious to have people living in the real estate development he had started out on the very edge of town. I remember the few scattered houses, the muddy new streets, the sparseness of trees, the high grass in the vacant meadows between the new buildings, and a solid bank of trees in the distance beyond. I attended the Dundee school, a new brick building about a mile away, but less than half when you cut across the rolling meadows which, but a short time before, had been cow pastures. Dad would take me to school in the morning and I would return home on the streetcar or, when weather was nice, I might walk home across the fields.

I recall one afternoon how vast the world seemed as I trudged along the old cow path. When the land dipped between the green hills I could see nothing but the sky above, and the only sound was a small metallic click that seemed to follow me. When I paused, to see if it might be an insect noise, the sound stopped, yet started again when I resumed walking. I looked around me curiously—nothing moved in the meadow, no human or animal presence shared with me what seemed to be unbounded space. Even the sky above me was empty of clouds. Only the sun, moving toward the western horizon, occupied the vault of heaven as I walked along.

I was almost home when, looking down at my feet, I uncovered the mystery of the clicking sound—it was made by the metal tips of my shoelaces tapping against the metal eyelets of my high topped shoes. Relieved and amused, I arrived home feeling like an explorer who has crossed the jungle veldt unscathed. I told Dad about the incident next Sunday morning on the way to church.

For over a year now I had been Dad's acolyte, going with him to each morning service when he would serve Communion. It was a quiet, almost intimate experience with just the two of us behind the altar rail. I, in my red cassock, white surplice and Buster Brown collar, would bring him the cruets from which he would fill the chalice with water and wine; then the small box from which he would take the wafers to consecrate as the Bread of Life.

"How many?" Dad would whisper to me, and I, having counted the number of parishoners in the church during the early part of the service while Dad was facing the altar reading the prayers, would whisper back to him, "Ten", or "Twelve," or whatever number of the faithful as had come out in the early hours to share the Lord's Supper in those small churches to which my Dad ministered. I loved the crinkling smile of his eyes behind the pince–nez glasses. Those were moments when I felt very close to my father. I never thought about it then, but Dad must have enjoyed having his oldest son with him in the chancel. I have wondered since if he had dreams of my possibly following him in his chosen profession? But he never intimated it to me then, and I had never had a chance, in my later teens, to have such adult discussions with him.

However, that morning in Omaha, as the streetcar clanged along in the early dawn, I told Dad about my walk home across the meadows and the mystery of the clicking sound that followed me. Dad understood my sense of uneasiness and my feeling of minor triumph when I uncovered the cause. Then, as he often did with me, he used the experience as a spiritual analogy to help me understand the intangible. This small ticking noise, Dad explained, was like the presence of God. God was always with me, even when I could not hear Him. I should always remember that and call upon Him through prayer when I needed help.

"But if God is with me all the time," I asked Dad, "why do I have to go to church to find Him?"

Dad chuckled at that, for he had a fine sense of humor. Then he explained that we simply went to church in order to learn more about God and to thank Him for our blessings by singing praises to Him. That seemed to make sense and so I accepted it, but from that day on I ceased to think of God as residing solely within the buildings we called churches. I guess it was the beginning of my serious awareness of God's presence as a personal entity I could reach out to.

But it was not until some three years later when I was almost twelve that I had an experience of direct confrontation with God. It happened when our baby sister, Louise, died.

It is not my purpose in this book to give a chronological biography of all that has happened in my life. That would take a much larger volume and defeat the purpose of this work, which is concerned primarily with my personal relationship to God. But, since it is impossible for me to explain the Divine presence in a philosophical vacuum as some writers do, I can only interpret God from where I have found Him as life has unfolded before me. With this purpose in mind I shall refer to only such events in my life as may be necessary to give the reader a picture of the position from which I have reached out to communicate with the Divine source of creation.

* * *

There was nothing dour or hidebound about Dad's religion. It was a thing of joy to him and he hoped that by it he could bring pleasure into other people's lives. We children felt it and our home life, though simple by monetary standards, was cheerful and bright. Dad and Mother never quarreled (at least not openly) and when my mother once again decided to take up a theatrical career in addition to raising us children (there were five of us now) Dad readily agreed, for he saw no conflict between the pulpit and the footlights. On the strength of Mother's earlier stage appearances under Fred Belasco at San Francisco's Alcazar Theater (before she married Dad) she now was accepted as a member of the resident stock company at Omaha's Brandeis theater. Soon she was a featured player and even we kids made our stage debuts in a play called *Mrs. Wiggs and the Cabbage Patch.*

Before long Mother's performances brought offers of a Broadway contract. Dad encouraged her to accept and go to New York.

"It's a great opportunity, Mary," he told her. "Put the children in a creche and go. I'll ask the bishop for a parish in the east. It will take some time, but we can join you there in a year or two."

Whether Mother was reluctant to leave us or afraid to go alone was never clear. But she turned down the Broadway offer. Soon after, in the spring of 1914, Dad accepted a call to a parish in Denver, Colorado.

Dad became assistant to the dean of Denver's Episcopal Cathedral. It was the largest and most prosperous of the parishes Dad had served. We had a nicer home and lived better than ever before. Dad was in charge of the youth work and he was in his element, for he loved that phase of his ministry. Mother, too, was very happy for she resumed her part-time theatrical career by joining the stock company at Denver's famous Elitche's Gardens. During this time she met Eddie Foy who was touring with his well-known vaudeville act, "Eddie Foy and the Seven Little Foys." Our two families became friends.

One day Eddie asked Mother and Dad if they would consider letting our youngest brother, four-year-old Teddy, join the Foy troupe. The youngest Foy child was growing too big to be carried on stage in the valise, which was a high point in the act, so they needed a replacement.

Once more, Mother's dream of the professional theatre had beckoned, but she wouldn't tolerate the notion of splitting up the family. However, I think that was the point in Mother's life when she decided that if Eddie Foy could do it with seven, she could do it with five, and come hell or high water she would not rest until she took her own brood to Broadway.

It was a strange, three-way conflict of obsession within my mother that ruled much of our lives in the immediate years ahead—Mother's frustrated ambition for a stage career, her fierce possessive love for her children, and her abnormal distaste for the manner by which we were created. This last obsession, I learned in later years, was like a poison in her system that finally completely corroded her relationship with father. Mother adored children, but hated sex. She told us often, when we were in our teens, that God should have found a better way to bring new life into this world, and she was not about to forgive Him for it.

Looking back some six decades later, while reading through Mother's letters and papers after her death, I have come to the conclusion that our parents had a deep and tender love for each other—a love so strong that it rode out storms which would have wrecked many weaker marriages. But I have a feeling that Mother married Dad partly because he was a priest, and she thought that a man concerned with spiritual things would be above the earthly passions of manhood. Such a sad perversion of normal healthy attitudes.

I think I was becoming unconsciously aware of this tension between Mother and Dad when my little sister was born in Chicago some two years later. Dad had left the Denver Cathedral at the end of a year because puritanical parishoners objected to the theatrical activities of the wife of their assistant curate. Dad bought our first automobile, a 1916 Maxwell touring car. We piled it high with camping equipment and as the April snows lingered on the mountainsides, we headed east through Nebraska toward Chicago and New York.

In those days there were no paved highways, only scraped gravel roads between cities, and it was considered courageous adventuring for a family to drive cross-country. It took us almost a month to cover the 1,000 miles to Chicago. There our money ran out and Dad secured the pastorate of two small churches in the suburbs of West Pullman and Roseland. It was there, in February of 1917, that my little sister Louise was born, and there, eight months later, she died of pneumonia. Five years younger than her brother Teddy, Louise was the caboose that ended our family train. That Mother loved her passionately, once she had arrived, was in keeping with her outsized affection for all her children. But something my sister Isobel said once indicated that Mother blamed Dad for having brought about this added mouth to be fed.

On the night that Louise lay in her crib, struggling for each breath, I went out into the yard of our house and began praying aloud to God to let her live. I said all the prayers I had been taught to use in church and Sunday School. Then I went back into the house. Louise had stopped breathing. Mother, who had little respect for the medical profession, had finally let Dad call for a doctor.

I went outside once more, and looking up to the star-filled heavens began praying again desperately, pleading for God to let my little sister live. I told God that since I was an acolyte, who served at His altar, I felt that should guarantee me special favor from the Almighty. "Please, please let Louise live!" Thus I kept on appealing to the night sky until the doctor arrived. I went back in then, and watched in numbed silence as the doctor made his examination. Mother went into hysterics and Dad sent us all to bed.

Two days later we went to the cemetery in a single black automobile. Just Dad and the three oldest children—sister Isobel, myself and next brother Tupper. Dad held the small white coffin on his lap and his face held such deep sadness that my heart ached for him. As we drove along he tried, with brief sentences, to explain to us the meaning and purpose of life. I don't remember just what he said; my mind was too full of disappointment that God had not answered my prayers. At the cemetery we three children stood beside the little grave and cried as Dad said a simple prayer. Then it was over and we walked back to the car. I turned for one more look at the grave and noted that it was at the edge of the cemetery and that a railroad track ran beside it. I was to note in later years, in two other distant cities, that the graves of our mother and our father were also at the edge of a cemetery along which ran railroad tracks. If there is any symbolism in that coincidental set of circumstances, I take it to be that our loved ones have continued on to a destination we cannot see, but it is a goal as purposeful as the rails laid down to reach it.

On that day in Chicago I watched my father's face as he joined us at the car. It was still as deeply sad as on the drive out, though now when he paused to wipe his glasses and his eyes I was sure he glanced upward for a moment, gratefully, as though recognizing a friend. He got into the car and I raised my own eyes to that unresponsive sky. Somehow I had an eerie feeling that God was watching this bit of earth whether we acknowledged Him or not. Though certainly at that moment, in my eleventh year, I was puzzled and spiritually dissatisfied with the explanations which organized religion had put forth on the subject of life and death. I had called on God and He had not answered. I was angry with Him. But I was also distressed with myself for my own inability to communicate with Him.

So, from the beginning, God became an ever growing concern in my life. Yet, though His form was often vague and His personality changed as my own perceptions grew, I learned to talk with Him. At first I had spoken through formal prayers. But after Louise died they gradually lost meaning for me because of their impersonal, stylized wording. Eventually, going beyond that point, my prayers became conversation. Sometimes it was casual, then again desperately earnest (though I did not shake my fist at God) as the revelations and involvements of life swept by, or over, me. But talk I did.

* * *

I believe conversation really began when I was fifteen. It was late August of 1921, and I was ending my second year as bugler at Owassippi, one of the three Chicago Boy Scout camps near Muskegon, Michigan. For a boy who hated city life, those golden summers had been pure treasure. I think I had never before felt so free and untroubled.

We were sitting around the campfire one night in the deep scented pine forest. The boys had finished singing "Clementine" and now we launched into our favorite, multi-versed ballad about the "Galloping Ship for an Ocean Trip..." Bullfrogs in the swamp on the other side of the hill, not to be outdone, added their haunting chords to the night's serenade and, as the melody lofted joyously into the moonlit sky a whippoorwill, somewhere beyond the firelight's circle, joined in the chorus. At that moment I felt a tap on my shoulder and turned to discover one of the camp's young staff directors motioning me to silence and to come with him.

Quietly, we departed the campfire circle. When well out of earshot we left the trail and moved deeper into the forest before he stopped to speak. Since as bugler I was the most junior staff member, I presumed he had instructions about my duties. I was not prepared for what followed.

"You have been 'tapped-out' to become a member of the Order of the Arrow," he said, "but you must first undertake the 'Ordeal.' From this moment until Retreat Formation tomorrow evening, you will speak to no one

under any circumstance. Go to your tent now and get a
canteen, a hand ax and a blanket. No flashlight. Avoid-
ing all personnel you will walk out from camp on the
northeast trail for one hour. Then find a spot off the
trail and make a fire, using only these two matches. Sit
beside it for at least two hours in meditation. Think
deep about the Scout Oath and Law, about what you
will do with your life, about service to others. Think
about God."

After that, he said, I could sleep, but must return to
camp at dawn. Still speaking to no one I would go to
the mess hall where I would serve my fellow scouts all
day in silence. At Retreat, the Camp Director would
release me.

"Are you willing to undertake this Ordeal of Service?" the young counselor now asked me.

Assuring him I was ready, I proceeded as he had
directed me. Moving away from camp I found the
trail—alternately moonlit or darkly tunneled through
the close pressing forest. It must have been near on to
eleven when I finally stopped, left the trail, and started
my fire. I had seen no houses, no light from distant
windows. I had passed no human being on my long
walk through the night. I was alone. Sitting with my
back against a rough-barked pine tree and looking into
the fire's wavering flames, I began my first serious attempt to talk directly with God.

At first I thought about my participation in the Scout
program. The importance of personal responsibility under the Oath and Law was a matter of very solemn
concern to me. That I should be selected by my fellow
campers for membership in the recently created Scout

fraternity, The Order of the Arrow, indicated that I must somehow be succeeding in that responsibility. Now I would be given additional trusts for which to be accountable. The Order of the Arrow, created by Dr. E. Urner Goodman, Scout Director of Philadelphia's Treasure Island Camp, was built on an impressive legend of the Delaware Indian Tribe. It was dedicated to preserving the best traditions of wilderness camping and to encouraging the performance of service to others.

I thought, now, about the Order's Indian ceremonies which I had heard other Scouts discussing, though only in vague detail because they were considered secret, reserved only to members of the Order. But I knew they would have very special significance for me because I bore Indian genes in my body. On my father's side my quarter-blood Indian grandmother traced her lineage directly to the tribe of Powhatan, whose people had such important influence upon the English settlers at Jamestown a little over three hundred years ago. Those Indians had sat at their campfires, too, conferring through song and ceremony with their God, Manitou. But wasn't He the same Divine Being my mind now reached out to talk to? If, as the Bible proclaimed, there was only one God, Creator of Heaven and Earth, then Manitou, the God of my Indian ancestors had to be the same.

Looking up at the night sky I saw the stars taking over the dome of infinity from the setting moon. I knew from my studies of astronomy that they, including the millions I could see and the billions I could not see, had been there long before my Indian forebears and even before their ancestors, farther back than recorded time. Those stars and everything upon which they had been shining for all those eons were God's creations, even as I and the pinewood crackling in the fire at my feet had to also be His. My reason insisted there could be only one God. He had created the universe—the galaxies, the sun and our planet earth. It was good, and I was glad to be a part of it.

My heart swelled and I tried to tell God how grateful I was, how beautiful I found His world to be...then I faltered and couldn't, for my mind had run smack into a very formidable obstacle. It had been planted in my subconscious by words from Scripture I'd heard often in church, the statement by Jesus of Nazareth, "My kingdom is not of this world," and the sad lament of St. Paul, "Save us from this evil world in which we live,"—phrases that seemed to discredit Divine purpose in creating this planet Earth. I shook my head and tried to resume the conversation.

"Does that mean, God, that your creation of this world was a mistake? Why did you give up?"...My conversation stumbled, and God didn't help me out with an answer. Perhaps He was as confused as I by the contradictions that man puts together inside the beautiful buildings which he raises up to be his churches, which he solemnly dedicates to the honor and glory of God, then establishes contradictory doctrines to deny Him.

Right then I felt that something was wrong about man's relationship to the God who created him. Was the God above my campfire, to Whom I now felt so close, the same as the God who presided over the altars of the churches in whose shadows I had been raised? Somehow I couldn't reconcile the two. The one was vast—as difficult to define as the illimitable universe He had created, but as purposeful as the rising sun. The other was limited by the boundaries of a creed. Lord of a vague other world which offered no recognizable objective. A God who disavowed this small planet on which we live and promised to save us from it.

My campfire burned low. I put some more wood on it and smiled ruefully to myself when the shower of sparks, as explosive as my thoughts, leaped up to challenge the dark sky above. My talk with the Infinite had retreated into a troubled dialogue with myself. Maybe, I thought, the fault was my own. Maybe I didn't understand the full meaning of what I'd learned about God during all those hundreds of hours I'd spent reverently moving about in the many churches where my father ministered or in the schools where the gentle nuns and kindly priests had taught. I respected the sincerity of their faith in God as they knew Him. I loved them, especially my Dad, for the love they had shown to others and to me. But I knew now, just as surely as I could feel the soil under the tree where I sat, that I could never again accept the precepts of their theology which looks upon this world of God's creation as a place of evil. If things here were not good, then somehow we must have misinterpreted God's purpose here.

Wrapping my blanket tightly around my shoulders, I settled down against the roots of the pine tree and exchanged grateful sleep for disquieting thoughts. Before the sun rose I was up again and on my way back to camp. The vigorous walking warmed my cold-stiffened muscles, while the sights and sounds of the wakening woodland soothed my troubled mind. Yes—the world He had made was indeed good. I would cling to that certainty.

Some readers may feel that I could not have thought this through at that early age of my life, that what I am putting down now is partly the thinking of later, more mature years—perhaps, but who is to say? Yet this much I do know: a part of that campfire talk with my Creator is still with me now, even as are also the long-ago musings of my Indian ancestors beside their lodge fires and of my Scottish progenitors beside the smoky peat fires in their Highland crofts. I am the continuation of an endless evolution. All this is with me—in me—in my genes—in the dark recesses of my brain from which I daily draw inspiration. They, and I, are part of a Divine plan that has to do with this planet and the galaxy within which it orbits. I knew that night, as I first tried to talk with God, that I must continue the dialogue, and someday He would reveal that plan to me.

I would surely have shared this experience of spiritual questioning with Dad when I came home at the end of summer, but he was not there to talk to. In fact, Dad had not been home much for the past three years because, following a nervous breakdown, he had left the two parishes in south Chicago, worked at several secular jobs for a while, and then accepted a call to minister to a scattered group of churches in western Missouri and Kansas. It was a circuit-rider type of ministry with no home-based rectory from which to maintain a family, so we stayed in Chicago and Dad would come to visit us periodically.

I didn't understand exactly what was happening to our family. But my sister Isobel, a year and a half older than me and very close to Mother, evidently knew that there was growing rift between our parents. Isobel said mother had explained to her that Dad was emotionally ill after his breakdown, and it was best for him to be free of the responsibilities of a family—to be alone for awhile. And this appeared to be quite all right with Mother. She seemed to relish being in complete charge of her family. She became the editor of a labor-party newspaper, took vigorous part in union activities, and made dramatic speeches before the then striking South Chicago and Indiana steel mill workers.

On the scattered occasions when Dad would come home for a short visit, I was impressed with the sadness in his eyes, as had been on the occasion of Louise's death. Dad had always been kindly and gentle and he continued this way on his visits. But I was now more aware of his relationship with Mother and though she kept telling us kids Dad was still emotionally sick and seemed relieved after he was gone again, I thought of him as merely a very lonely man—and in the night I would pray for God to watch over him.

CHAPTER II

The Theatre Years:

Through God's Looking Glass

Thus was my life changing from its familiar pattern. The simple existence I had known as a clergyman's son had very recognizable boundaries—the modest rectory home, the church, the scout troop, the local school. These had been the common place limits of my daily experience.

Now, in my mid-teens, strange changes were tearing me from those unpretentious surroundings. The ragged years of a widening rift between my parents had gradually taken away our familiar Sundays. Without Dad's presence and his daily commitment to the needs of a particular congregation, regular church attendance fell by the wayside. Mother and sister stopped going altogether, though my young brothers still enjoyed the choirs of several nearby churches. But, for myself, since Scout activities had become a very big part of my life, I spent the weekends hiking and camping in the many forest preserves around Chicago.

It didn't look as if Dad and Mother were any nearer getting back together, for his visits became shorter and farther apart. He told us the bishop was pleased with his work because it was providing for the very real spiritual hunger of many widely scattered rural families. Mother seemed to agree with the bishop and, I thought, offered Dad no strong encouragement to stay with us.

After one short visit in the fall of 1922, I felt that my parents' separation was almost complete, for Dad, as he always did just before he left, talked with me briefly. But this time, instead of reminding me to be a good boy and obey Mother, he said, "I'm proud of you son, working to help with the family finances. (I had left high school to take a job as freight tracing clerk with the Santa Fe Railroad). You're a good boy, Starr. You're really the head of the family while I'm gone. Take care of them for me, son."

Then Dad kissed me, picked up his suitcase and walked away. My heart ached as I went back into the house. Mother had been watching us from the doorway. This time she wasn't crying as she often had before, but there was a strangeness in her eyes, almost as though she were looking far into the future.

"What did Papa say to you?" she asked me.

"He told me to be good and to take care of you," I replied. Mother held me tight against her apron, which smelled of flour and apples for she had been making pies.

"I'm sure you will always take your father's place," she said softly, and kissed me on the cheek. "Let us both pray that God will look after Papa—he needs caring for, too."

I was glad Mother said that, for I loved both my parents dearly. It is a traumatic experience, especially in the teen years, when children find their parents divided and they must try to show them both love without partiality. I wondered, then, why God allowed families to split up. And many times during that hectic period I would fling questions toward the unresponsive sky where I had been assured the Almighty resided, but from which direction, now, no replies seemed forthcoming. Perhaps this was so because life was moving very fast in those years and I did not realize that communication with God is best accomplished in moments of serenity. Surely this factor is borne out by the writings of sages and philosophers who for centuries have used various forms of meditation as an avenue of communication with the Source of Creation.

This time, as soon as Dad had left for Kansas, Mother began planning to move on to New York. Those last years in Chicago she had been very active in theatrical circles. She had short engagements with various local stock companies, and she cultivated friendships with several actors whose successful Broadway shows had, while touring, played Chicago theatres. Mother became a charter member of the first actors' union, the Actors Equity Association, when Equity called its first strike against the managers of Chicago's Loop theatres. Thus Mother's dream of Broadway was fed afresh. So, in the fall of 1922, without much planning and even less money, Mother took us five children and headed east. The journey took almost a year, with ill fated stock company engagements and vaudeville tries leaving us stranded for months in Pontiac, Michigan, and

Pittsburgh. But, by the next May, we had reached Philadelphia.

It was there, in that "City of Brotherly Love," that I saw Dad for the last time. He had come east to try for a reconciliation. But Mother, with her life's goal only a few miles away, was in no mood to cooperate. There were never any scenes between Mother and Dad—the furious currents which must have surged between them were deep down, and they never surfaced before us kids. The actual details of that last confrontation between our parents I never really learned about until many, many years later from sister. But I realize now that it was Mother's obsessive revulsion against the physical companionship of marriage. She saw no need to reintroduce Dad, again, into the intimacy of her home life. It was this rock upon which the bond between them was wrecked.

That summer I went back again to my job as bugler at the Michigan Scout Camp. But Mother, sister and my younger brothers moved on to New York City. When I joined them there, in late August of 1923, they had already established our home in a fourth floor walk-up apartment on west 43d Street, in Manhattan. This area of seedy brownstones, popularly called "Hell's Kitchen," was chosen because rents were cheap and, being just west of 8th Avenue, it was on the edge of the Broadway theatrical district, thus within easy walking distance of theatres and producers' offices. Getting theatrical parts meant long hours of tramping from agents' offices to producers' offices, sometimes to studios or theatres, following up tips on shows reported to be casting, maybe rehearsing, or only in initial stages being "readied." The procedure was known as "plugging." It might more appropriately have been called "plodding," because that's what it entailed—day after day, week after week, month after month. All actors, professional or amateur-hopefuls, did it. Only a small percentage of the profession, leading men and women and some top echelon actors who were much in demand, did not have to make-the-rounds.

Our family had already been making the rounds for many weeks, with only nominal results. But, Mother explained when I arrived, I would not have to do that, because she had already arranged, through a friend, a good office job for me with the Metropolitan Life Insurance Company. It would be steady employment (show jobs were not) and, Mother's friend assured me, I could work up the ladder with this big firm, eventually earning an executive position for myself. It was, he said, a really fine career to contemplate.

But that contemplation appalled me. I hated desk work. Pencils and paper, even at school, were like chains of the worst sort. I wanted to be out of doors. Even though the need to help with family support had forced me to go to work after my second year of high school, I had been reading avidly, preparing myself for a career in forestry. Now it appeared that family fortunes and circumstances were against me. In order to keep my promise to Dad to look after the family, I would be forced into a repugnant white-collar job in a Manhattan skyscraper. In desperation I appealed to Mother.

"Why can't I look for an acting job like my brothers?"

Mother hesitated. I was not considered to have any acting talent. On our journey east, in Pennsylvania, Mother had concocted a family vaudeville act, a dramatic skit. I, at 17, with the aid of makeup, was playing a man of about 35. The act was a disaster. The theatre manager advised Mother to have the act rewritten and re-cast. "Pep up the old man," he had said.

Mother shrugged, allowing I might give it a try for a few weeks. She sent me to the Lambs Club to see her friend Grant Mitchell. He in turn scribbled a note on his calling card and sent me to see his friend Walter Hampden at the National Theatre. Mr. Hampden, one of the most noted Shakespearean actors of the day, was in the final week of rehearsal for his production of *Cyrano de Bergerac*. He gave me a bit part—one line— and multiple costume changes as a citizen, a pastry cook and a Gascoyne Cadet. In another week the play opened. Brian Hooker's magnificent blank verse translation of Edmund Rostand's dramatic classic took New York by storm. "Cyrano" was a smash hit, destined to run for almost two years. For better or worse I was launched as an actor.

That fall the rest of the family also secured theatrical engagements, and mother was convinced our fortunes were made. But the game is not that easily conquered. Salaries, except for the stars and leads, were low. Our food and lodging were no better than during the rectory years, though the excitement and glamour made our life seem to move on a higher plane.

In those days, popular myth attributed to actors a bohemian disregard for religion and moral values. But I found theatrical folk no different in their hungers than ordinary citizens. All were reaching out for spiritual nourishment. Only in the make-believe world of the theatre, with its unconventional background there is, perhaps, greater opportunity for the development of nonconformist thought in philosophical matters. This factor, combined with a great deal of steadfast devotion by many actors to traditional religious creeds, produces a community keenly aware of the presence of God.

Indeed, the reality of Divine presence is so generally accepted in the professional theatre that I felt no estrangement in this new environment, and my search continued for answers to why God had placed us here on this planet. While religious values still guided our lives, we seldom went to church anymore. Perhaps Mother's differences with Dad had left her with a guilty feeling which caused her, now, to stay away.

While my mind had begun to reject many of the tenants of modern Christian thinking, I still missed the closeness of spirit with my father—those Sunday mornings when we would be up before dawn and off in the semi-darkness to conduct a series of communion services. While we did not carry on much conversation there was always a warm comradeship between us, as we put on our vestments together in the tiny room at the side of the altar. How I wished we could have been together like that now. What wonderful conversations we could have had over the conflicts of spirit which were assailing me. But Dad died of a broken heart in October of 1923. He was alone in Kansas and we were far away in New York.

The news was a terrible shock to all of us. Mother took to her bed in a torrent of uncontrolled hysterics that lasted for several days and actually made her ill. That remorseful sorrow kept her in bed in that window-less, back bedroom of our 4th floor flat for a number of weeks. Looking back later with the knowledge born of accumulated experience, I feel certain that the shock had brought on, in a rather violent fashion, the change of life which all women go through. Thus was Mother finally rid of the God-created urge to perpetuate the species—the implementation of which had caused her so much unhappiness, but the results of which she had found so filled with an out-reaching love, yet had never learned how to adequately cope with.

For my younger brothers the sorrow was not deep because they could scarcely remember our actual rectory years. It is difficult for me to assess exactly how sister really felt because she had for so long been influenced by Mother, yet I knew she genuinely loved Dad's gentle disposition and grieved now that it was gone forever.

For myself, a light had gone out that could not be re-lit. The light was in the smiling eyes I loved and the sadness in those eyes these recent years had hurt me profoundly. Had I known at the time of Dad's death what I learned years later, I would have been even more distraught. For when Dad came to Philadelphia in early summer, Mother had refused his request that he be allowed to take me with him to his class reunion at Suwanee, Tennessee. It was at that famous university's divinity school that he had earned his master's in theology. Oh, how I would have loved that—what a wonderful time it could have been for both of us. But it never happened and I never knew at the time that it could have been.

Though the nature of youth seldom dwells long on bereavement, Dad's loss stayed sharply with me for over a year and, in a very poignant way, motivated, a lengthy discourse with my Creator on the subject of death.

The dramatic sweep of Rostand's *Cyrano de Bergerac* was heady fare for a neophyte actor's first Broadway experience. I loved the play and, night after night, during the magical third and fifth acts (in which I did not appear) I would stand in the wings, just to watch. Eventually, I could recite, by heart, every line in the play. The fifth, the last, was my favorite. Here, at day's end, under the wide spreading branches of a tree in a Convent Garden, Cyrano, mortally wounded by an assassin, comes once more to visit Roxanne, the exquisite intellectual lady whom he has secretly loved all of his life. Seated under the tree she is busily engaged with her embroidery. Cyrano, his bandaged head covered by the flamboyant Gascon's hat, with its white plume of honor accenting each move of his proud face, sits down to resume for Roxanne his daily recounting of the current Paris scene. A breeze rustles through the tree and its autumn-colored leaves begin descending gently on the couple below. A chapel bell tolls and the voices of nuns are heard singing a litany.

Cyrano speaks: "The leaves—"
Roxanne, picking up his thoughts, "What color—perfect Venetian red: Look at them fall."

"Yes," replies Cyrano, "they know how to die. A little way from the branch to the earth, a little fear of mingling with the common dust—and yet they go down, gracefully—a fall that seems almost like flying."

Performance after performance, the beauty of those lines touched like a balm my own saddened heart, until, one night, the fact of death seemed no longer a burden but rather a peaceful conclusion to nature's purposeful cycle. At that moment, the channel of communication was once again open between God and myself and I ventured to question:

"Since you, Lord, created everything, then nature's laws are really God's commandments, are they not? Nature isn't some separate entity, concerned only with visible elements of this earth's geography and ecology, but rather Mother Nature, as we call her, is actually the revelation of Your smile. Nature is this planet's evidence of the Divine force that moves the Universe, and that was what You were trying to reveal to me that night in the Michigan forest, wasn't it? Well, I think I understand it now. But why, then, does the Christian church insist that you have conquered death? You, God, created death. You gave it a primary mission in Your ever-evolving universe. You don't have to overcome death at all, do You? It's we who have to overcome fear of it, to learn to know death as part of Your reason for our being here on earth."

The spell of that moment of discourse was intense. I was lifted out of myself, out of the theatre. I felt I was standing on the brink of a tremendous void beyond which a great discovery waited. Then I was jolted, physically, and my attention returned to the theatre. The stagehand who had touched me was taking hold of the ropes to draw the final curtain. On stage Cyrano, his back to the tree, was lashing out with his sword in a last duel with his old enemies—pride, prejudice, envy and vanity. The spell of communication with the Divine returned for a flashing instant of revelation, and I knew that I, myself, would have to do battle with those same adversaries before I could understand the full meaning of God's purpose for us here on earth.

In the sixty years since I watched the leaves fall in that last act of *Cyrano,* I have seen thousands upon thousands of thousands more dropping to earth in forests, parks and farm lands. In like manner, I have watched the passing of treasured members of my own family, and the tragic deaths of so many of my military comrades on the battlefield. But always, since then, it has been with a feeling of gentle goodbye, knowing that earthly completion has been a vital, necessary part of a mighty celestial process—the secret to which I am certain I will someday be given the key. As my good friend Ralph Lankler expressed so well, "Death is but a horizon, and the horizon is but the point to which the eye can see."

This philosophical resolution within my mind on the subject of God's purpose in establishing death proved a springboard to further debate with the Creator. I remember one day standing on 43d street, just off Broadway, with Mother. We had stopped to say hello to a dear old clergyman, the Rev. Mr. Hall, who lived in our area. This sprightly, septuagenarian Episcopal priest, who had been a seminary friend of my father's, used to conduct impromptu open-air preaching at noontime on Wall Street in Manhattan's financial district. Today he was telling Mother, "Your sons, Mrs. Jones, should be in the ministry, like their Dad."

"Father Hall," Mother replied, "I think they can do just as much good for the Lord outside the church. You realize, don't you, that there's only a very fine line between the pulpit and the footlights."

The old gentleman's eyes twinkled. "Perhaps you're right, perhaps you're right. Well, I'll be watching for them."

And off he went about his business, a ray of ecclesiastical sunshine in a black suit and a bowler hat.

Mother said nothing to me on the subject, and I did not pursue it. But I noticed that she looked at me several times in an odd way. Was she thinking, perhaps, to make amends for Dad's death by persuading me to join the ministry? Of course, she knew I had never been inclined to the pulpit as a career. But of course, my taking to the footlights had only been an accident of flight. Anyway, I decided I'd better be ready to protect myself. So, from that day on, I was marshaling, in my mind, an enumeration of the obstacles I found to a logical acceptance of Christian theology.

Thus I began to re-read the New Testament. Now, I discovered that the Gospel according to Saint John differed radically from the Gospels of Matthew, Mark and Luke. These three had reported, if sometimes contradictorily, on the public life of Jesus of Nazareth—where he went, what he said and what he did. These Gospels revealed a kindly man. A Teacher, who with simple parables, showed us that when we actively love our fellow-man we are keeping the Second Great Commandment, thereby fulfilling that supreme injunction without which we, as mortals, are unable to understand and implement the First. And throughout his ministry the Gospels of Matthew, Mark and Luke revealed Jesus as an individual who did not emphasize himself, but rather God the Father.

However, the Gospel of John did something entirely different. It took Jesus' words and deeds and out of them created a dogmatic theology. John phrased these words in such a context that, for me, they represented a very rough road to rational thought. And it is the Gospel of John upon which so much of the Christian faith is built! What particularly bothered me in the writing of John's Gospel was his emphasis on the personal pronoun "I," which thus created the image of an authoritarian Jesus that is in sharp contrast to the man of gentle humility pictured by the Gospels of Matthew, Mark and Luke.

It was only many years later, when I learned that the Gospel of St. John was written a great number of years after the Crucifixion, that I realized how much editoralizing must have taken place. And my mental dissatisfaction between these two conflicting personalities of Jesus was not resolved until many years after that, while I was creating International Editions for *Guideposts* magazine. A decidedly unorthodox, but truly logical, insight came to me when I was discussing the interfaith policy of *Guideposts* with a very perceptive Hindu gentleman from Bombay. But the telling of it belongs to my later commuting years.

Debating these contradictions in my continuing discourse with God, I put it this way,

"Tell me, God, if Jesus were divine, as claimed by the Gospel of John, how could such a death have value as a sacrifice?

Death of a person who is divine and will live again is no great sacrifice at all. I've known men in battle who had no hope of any other life whatever to quickly give up that one life in order to save another. Now that is genuine heroic sacrifice. But for a divine individual, possessed of more than one life, to claim a single death experience as worthy sacrifice is being guilty of bogus heroics, isn't that true?

"If, on the other hand, Jesus were not divine, but simply human—the humble, much-loved carpenter of Nazareth, then such a sacrificial death to propitiate your anger, God, because of human sinfulness, serves only to accuse your Divinity of pettiness. Didn't those writers of the Gospels get off the track a bit? While the Christian theology condemned human sacrifices of the early, so-called pagans and the animal sacrifices of the Hebrews, didn't the Christian church fall into the same trap with the glorification of a crucifixion? Any way you look at it, the theology of death on a cross to ensure man's soul a place in the afterworld defies logical thought and says little for the majesty of a God of Love. So, there you have it, Lord. Now lead me, please, to some logical answers!"

So much for my study of Scripture. As it turned out, no effort was made by Mother to induce me to enter the ministry. Thus, my marshaling of objections served little purpose other than to increase my hunger for a more satisfying spiritual nourishment than I had found, up to that point in my life, within conventional Christian boundaries. So, in the years ahead, I browsed, also, in the pastures of other philosophies—some recognized as religious, others merely as compilations of moral principles—and in some I found much sustenance.

About this time my career took another accidental turn. After two years with Walter Hampden in *Cyrano* and *Othello* and a season with Eugene O'Neill's *Great*

God Brown, I was invited to take part in a benefit performance at the Commodore Hotel where the Theatre Guild was staging its "Tapestry Ball." Someone had heard that I did American Indian dances and I was asked if I would put on "my Indian act" for that occasion. Well, I had no act, as such. My Indian lore was mainly a hobby, evolved from my love for the culture of my ancestors. Their dances were not creations intended to entertain, but serious interpretations of their relationship with life and nature.

However, such explanations had little meaning for the theatrical entrepreneurs who were putting on the Commodore gala which would raise funds for the purchase of two huge tapestries, designed to adorn the auditorium walls of the new Guild Theatre now being built on 52d Street west of Broadway.

"Couldn't you put on a war dance for us?" I was asked. "We've seen pictures of your costume—it's stunning!"

The costume, which consisted only of moccasins, breech-cloth and a magnificent Sioux eagle-feather bonnet, won the argument. I put together some of the most dramatic dance steps I had learned in my research, and on the evening of the ball performed, if not with too much authenticity at least with great vigor, on the improvised stage built at one end of the great ballroom. I finished the dance with a running leap that carried me out of sight, through the curtained wings, and off the edge of the stage platform beyond. When I climbed back up and limped onto the stage for my curtain call, I did not realize then that the painful leap was actually the first tremor of a shake-up in my career. Of such vagaries are theatrical decisions made, and the shadows of coming events cast before us.

Some months later I began rehearsing for George Bernard Shaw's *Caesar and Cleopatra,* the play which would open the new Guild Theatre. I had a small part as the boatman, and my youngest brother, Ted, was playing Ptolomy, the Egyptian boy-king who was the brother of the fabled Cleopatra. It was in that part, as Cleopatra, that a promising young actress, Miss Helen Hayes, was to achieve stardom.

As soon as the play opened, the Theatre Guild began putting together an intimate musical revue with some actors who had been appearing in various Guild shows. All were young and all unknown, as also were the revue's composer and lyricist, a team who, up to then, had been writing music and lyrics for Yale University's Triangle shows—Richard Rogers and Lawrence Hart. The Guild's musical revue was *The Garrick Gaieties,* and among its other then unknowns, were Lee Strassberg, Phillip Loeb, Lillian Roth, Romney Brent, Sterling Holloway, June Cochran and Edith Mizner. Because of my Indian leap I was offered the featured dance number to be performed for the first time on Broadway, the famous Mexican hat dance, the Jarabe Tapatio. My dance partner in this colorful folk number was Rose Rolando the beautiful fiery wife of Tatanacho, one of the heroes of the Mexican Revolution which was then drawing to a climax below the Rio Grande. For me the chance was the beginning of a long-lasting love for Mexican people and their culture, which, some 50 years later, would finally take me to

Mexico where I would write an inspired play about the early religious conflicts which had sparked the long drawn-out Mexican Revolution. How strange, sometimes, are the early tracings of the paths along which our lives will later move.

The successful *Garrick Gaieties* ran for over a year. For me, it was the first of many Broadway musicals that would follow—*Circus Princess, Blonde Sinner, Take the Air* and *Girl Crazy,* each one challenging my talents to make the event of the moment a meaningful milestone in my accidental career. Yet, though I enjoyed each show—as who wouldn't with music, laughter, audience acclaim, and enthusiastic people to work with—it was great fun, but, as time went on, I was not satisfied. I felt there should be more purpose to life than just succeeding at any job that came my way.

Perhaps this discontent had its roots in the continuing discourse with my Creator for, just prior to the musical-comedy phase of my life, there had been some rather intense give-and-take on that particular subject. It was one of the lines in *The Great God Brown* that touched off this round of contention. This was the play Eugene O'Neill wrote in which the actors wore masks denoting their true or false selves, as the world might see them. In the last act of the play, the successful architect, William A. Brown, has just hidden the body of his nemesis, Dion. He goes to the outer office to meet Dion's wife, Margaret, and some men who have to come to approve Dion's plan for a new Capital Building. In a frenzy of jealousy, Brown tears the plans to pieces, then rushes off, only to return in a moment wearing the mask of Dion, whose personality he has assumed. Dion speaks:

> "Everything is all right—all for the best—you mustn't get excited! A little paste, Margaret! A little paste, gentlemen! And all will be well! Life is imperfect, Brothers! Men have their faults, Sister! But with a few drops of glue much may be done!"...He edges toward the door...his fingers to his lips. "Ssssh! This is Daddy's bedtime secret for today: Man is born broken. He lives by mending. The Grace of God is glue!"

Those last three short sentences had a beautiful sound that charmed the ears and a poetic ring of truth to them. But on later analysis, they sparked heated debate. At least they did for me, and for many in the audience. I know, because the management of the play held a number of discussion seminars with the cast and the audiences following some of the Wednesday matinee performances.

All members of the cast were invited to participate in the informal discussions about what author O'Neill meant by this or that line or the oft-confusing use of masks. It is interesting to note that in this drama, Dion's sons (played by my three brothers and myself) represented characters too young, yet, to have developed dual personalities, so we wore no masks. Therefore, at the matinee seminars, we were seldom drawn into the conversations. Often only Kenneth McGowan, our director and one of our play's three producers, would be present to act as the seminar's moderator. This trio—Eugene O'Neill, Robert Edmund Jones and Kenneth McGowan (playwright, designer and director respectively)—were among the contemporary theater's most delightful gentlemen, and I use the term gentlemen in its highest connotation. For, while most theatrical producers are in the business either to make money or to satisfy personal ego, I observed that O'Neill, Jones, and McGowan were seriously concerned that their stage efforts should help society to better understand its mutual kinships, and to see these relationships, as it were, through what might be called "God's looking glass."

Well, regardless of other, perhaps more erudite, observations, I began to take exception to O'Neill's statement, "Man is born broken, he lives by mending. . ." I could understand that the playwright's statement of man's imperfection probably stemmed from O'Neill's early grounding in the precepts of Roman Catholicism which proclaims emphatically, as do also most Protestant churches, the doctrine of original sin. This harsh dogma insists that sinful man is doomed to die in that cursed, pre-birth status of imperfection with no hope for eternal life unless he will seek freedom from that inherited (through no fault of his own) scourge, by declaring belief in the name of Jesus Christ.

Such a clumsy premise defies logic, and I wrestled with God in so many words:

"When, in Your infinite wisdom, Lord, You created the universe and placed man on this small planet, in the galaxy we call the Milky Way, You must have placed him here for a specific purpose. Reason tells me this design is of tremendous magnitude, because You gave man the amazing creative authority of free will—the power to do whatever each individual may wish to do while living out his years here. Reason then suggests that Your motive for bestowing this awesome privilege has to mean that You expect each individual, during his or her years on this planet, to do something special with that moment in which they exist."

The thought was so lofty that it shook up all my previously arrived at spiritual horizons. And I argued insistently with God as to what it might be that solitary individuals like myself could have to contribute to a continuously evolving universe:

"What is it, Lord, that each of us has got which no other human being possesses?"

The question dogged my thinking, throwing its challenge at me from the face I looked at each night in the dressing room makeup mirror—and plaguing my daytime thoughts while walking on the streets, or as I would be working at acrobatic dance exercises on an empty stage, lit only be the single bulb of a worklight casting its shadowy illumination over empty stage and unoccupied auditorium alike. The magic of shadows—like music they evoke, they stimulate...often at such times I felt I was on the verge of discovering a momentous revelation about man's place in the cosmos.

As my arguments with the Infinite continued, my dissatisfaction with O'Neill's philosophy grew. I decided that, however beautifully he had phrased it, his depiction of men as being "born broken" was denial of perfection in Divine creation. It was, quite simply, illogical. Thus, likewise, I came to reject the premise of Holy Scriptures that man is born under the blight of "original sin." That negative and uncomplimentary idea accused the Creator of being a vengeful, spiteful God, one who would carry a grudge through untold centuries. I found the implication unworthy of mature thinking. For years that unpalatable thought had set like a lead weight in my metaphysical stomach. Now it gave me spiritual indigestion—so I vomited it up.

"The theory of original sin," I now told the Lord, "defies sound reasoning. I see no logic in it."
"And just what do you see?" was the question God pressed back at me.
A fair enough riposte, I thought, so I parried. "I see individual man as God's creation, endowed with amazing energy, skill, capability. I see man as possessing the spark of Your divine power."
"Power for doing what?"
"I have been asking You that, Lord. I thought You would show me what man is supposed to do."
"What do you think man can do?"
"Anything his mind may conceive of, really. As far as I can see no one has ever yet been able to calculate a limit to what man's brain can accomplish."
"And why should that be so?"
"Because man's brain, his mind, is the product of Your Divine creation, Lord."
"And what is in that brain?
"Surely, the accumulation of all that man's ancestors have learned and experienced. Dim, perhaps, in some places, but most vivid from the genes of his closest progenitors, his parents and grandparents."
"And, to that total each individual can then supply—what?"
The spirit of God was pressing me hard now. "His own experiences, Lord, which of course are influenced by the unpredictable events that unfold with each new day, and to which he must add his own participation, at that moment."
"And all of which produces?"
"Something new, Lord. Something which,"—I paused as the enormity of the thought took hold of me..."something which, —never happened before in all of eternity, Lord!"
"And why is that so completely unique?"

"Because each of us adds that spark of divinity, from within himself, which he alone possesses, and which is utterly different from that in any other individual in the universe."

The day this thought took hold of me caused a revolution in my spiritual thinking. At last I could begin to see purpose in God's placing man on this globe, and endowing him with unrestricted free will. God's universe had not been "finished in seven days" as the early writers of the Bible had envisioned. It was still going on, still in the process of evolution. God was using man to continue that creation. And for that task God had entrusted man with amazing powers—God and men, together, were at work building life on this planet. And, since every human being is different, the result of each man's contribution has to be unique, because that result is totally unpredictable, even to God, until the very moment man makes his play.

Once this insight into Divine purpose was revealed to me, the entire span of my life took on new and vital meaning. Incidentally, this revelation came to me just prior to the stock market crash which began the Great Depression of the 1930s. The fact that it survived the difficulties of those days has proved to me its validity.

One other spiritual insight came to me out of my lengthy debate with God over the writings of Eugene O'Neill, I had told the Lord:

"Even if O'Neill's character in *The Great God Brown* had not propounded the premise that man is born broken and lives by mending, I still found that most of the characters in O'Neill's plays, no matter how beautifully drawn and adroitly presented, seemed unable to surmount their obstacles. To me O'Neill and his characters represented an attitude of futility in

man that I found distasteful." To which the Lord, in gentle
rebuke pressed back upon me with:

*"But aren't the successes of his plays an indication that
O'Neill's thoughts provide a form of satisfaction to many people, a form of gratification to their spiritual hunger?"*

Nourishment in pickles and vinegar? My mind rejected the formula. And then, the impromptu use of
food as a spiritual analogy struck me as a very realistic
way in which to look at, and accept, the wide variety of
religious thought abroad in the world today. All humans need food to keep our bodies alive. And we do
not fight among ourselves because some persons prefer
one sort of food and reject others. We respect the personal preference. In fact, if our minds or experience,
range worldwide, we learn that some people's bodies
thrive on certain foods which our own stomachs would
rebel at. Yet we do not try to convert those people to
change their eating habits and consume only the food
items we have found most suited to our own appetites
and bodies. Stomachwise, we are extremely liberal and
unprejudiced.

No battles are fought because most orientals prefer
rice to potatoes, or some African tribes find as much
nourishment and taste-bud satisfaction in eating insects
or rodents as perhaps we Americans find in hamburg-
ers and diet cola. We eat what appeals to us and respect the stomach dictates of others. I believe that the
same tolerance needs to be extended to all forms of
religious thought and practice, from any source which
provides satisfaction to the spiritual hunger of man.
Christian or Buddhist, Hebrew or Moslem, Hindu or
Confucian—we need to look upon them all as stock-

piles of spiritual nourishment. Once this thought is broadly accepted, how agreeable, then, could be man's sitting down together!

It is a provocative thought that people's souls can find refreshment from as wide a variety of religious beliefs as their bodies can find sustenance from almost any edible object! Thus it follows that any religious creed which helps people to live harmoniously together is good. This perception leads us, logically, to the realization that there should be no one universal religion for mankind, anymore than there can be only one food. It is the nature of the species, as God has created us. We need different foods for our bodies, and we need different spiritual nourishment for our souls.

Equally powerful is the thought that individuality is the priceless contribution each of us is privileged to make to this world.

Looking back now, I can see that these two stimulating ideas had worked themselves into the fabric of my subconscious to such an extent that they influenced much that I did in the next 12 years, before World War II and military service interfered, to somewhat direct my movements. The realization of Divine purpose in my individual, daily life now made every job effort that came my way seem important to work at, no matter how far it might lead me from what I felt were my special talents. Each new task became an adventure on the sea of God's continuing evolution.

In the matter of controlling your own life I recall vividly what happened to our family when the economic slump of the Great Depression decimated the New York theatre, and financing for new shows dried up the work source. Hundreds of actors gave up their profession all together. Those who hung on were able to do so only because they had some savings, or generous relatives, or temporary work as waiters and store clerks. Our family was no better off than most others, but we did have one asset most did not. We had a five-acre farm, 70 miles from the city, which we had purchased just six weeks before the stock market crash. There in our one-room cottage we could live rent free, while garden, cow and chickens would provide food. Since there was no work available on Broadway, we gave up our hotel apartment in Times Square and moved out to that small farm.

It was a period of struggle, but one of very warm family closeness. To raise cash we sold vegetables door-to-door in the nearby villages. Then, in the summer of 1934, with the Broadway stage still in the doldrums, we decided to make theatrical work for ourselves. By this time my two middle brothers were away on their own, but the remaining four of us (Mother, my sister, my youngest brother and myself) set about the task of creating a summer theatre stock company, one of the earliest of those depression inspired ventures which became known as the Straw-Hat Circuit.

We leased a large dairy barn on the State road just a mile from our farm. Oh, we had plenty of work then! I built a stage in the hay mow. We put in seats and box office, and Mother rounded up a company of out-of-work actors and started rehearsals. Brother Ted scoured the surrounding villages, summer homes and camps to create a subscription audience. Sister Isobel borrowed furniture and fixtures for the play's stage sets from our neighbors, and all of us played parts, leads or bits, as the situation demanded.

We played eight weeks that first summer to half empty houses; ten weeks the next summer to near capacity and, by the third summer, our Starlight Theatre season had extended to sixteen weeks and audiences filled the parking lot each night. Lowell Thomas, Elliot Roosevelt, Thomas Dewey and other famous residents of the area became regular weekly patrons. We had arrived.

Lowell Thomas became not only one of our foremost patrons at Starlight but also a kind and helpful friend. On opening night he was invariably there with several of his houseguests to welcome the new play. Once he brought Madame Chiang Kai-Shek, another time Gene Tunney. Frequently, Lowell would make an impromptu speech before the opening curtain, introducing to the audience the Broadway actors who brought their talents to our barn theatre for the entertainment of the Pawling-Quaker Hill community. Lowell was a very civic-minded individual.

While he maintained the privacy of his family life, at the same time Lowell would share with his neighbors the many notable people who were continually visiting him. He would draft these celebrities as players on his "Nine Old Men" softball team and they would play the local teams from Pawling Rubber Company; the teams of local farmers, store and bank clerks or the guards from Green Haven Prison. I played with the Nine Old Men one day along with New York drama critic Heywood Broun and U.S. Secretary of the Treasury Henry Morganthau.` Once, when Arctic explorer

Donald MacMillan was visiting the Thomases, Lowell invited everyone on The Hill to his barn studio so they could enjoy the personal films of MacMillan's North Pole voyages, narrated by the famous explorer himself.

Our Starlight Theatre continued for 30 years, with Isobel assuming managership after the war, when mother retired and Ted became a radio station director. I myself had left Starlight after the fifth summer, because the very close bond with mother had been disrupted when she took violent objection to a girl I wanted to marry.

However, before this breakup occurred, back in January of that year (1937), I appeared in what turned out to be my last Broadway play. I mention it here because something in the production had a spiritual impact on what I would later experience during World War II.

The Eternal Road was a most unusual play, written by Franz Werfel, with music by Kurt Weil and directed by the great Max Reinhardt. The mammoth drama was a saga of the endless persecution of the Jewish people from the time of Abraham up to Adolph Hitler. In essence, it was a litany of faith in God, of supplication to God. It was colorful history and magnificent spectacle—it should have run for five years, but it closed after only five and a half months. There were many reasons for this theatrical failure, some simply pragmatic, others I would call spiritual. Some, I think, are worth noting because, even now, 45 years later, the lessons are still valid.

On the practical side, *The Eternal Road* was a very expensive venture both to mount and to run. Since a large playing area was required, the old Manhattan Opera House on West 34th St. was chosen. The stage was rebuilt into a tremendous mountain, with a winding road and multiple-level playing spaces across its face. It was a gigantic set, worthy of Max Reinhardt and the biblical sweep of the story. Once opened, the weekly running expenses were large, too. It had a cast of well over 100, including Sam Jaffe, Byron Taylor, Lotte Lenya, Bertha Kunz-Baker and Ben Cutler in leading roles, while many lesser actors doubled in several parts. I played Issachar, one of Joseph's brothers, and the King's Messenger.

All of these high costs might have been amortized over a long run if the play itself had been successful. That it was not, I believe, was due to serious flaws in the creation of the production. First, from the standpoint of dramaturgy they attempted too much, with too many episodic scenes. By the time the fourth act rolled up over the mountain, the audience had lost track or wearied of the story. And, worst of all, the high spot of the drama came in the very first part of the play. The New York Times, in its review described that scene in these words:

> "The best part of *Eternal Road* occurred in the first act when Abraham, standing alone on the plain at the foot of the mountain, converses with God, whose voice answers him from the clouds. The dramatic impact of that scene would send chills up and down the spine of a marble column."

And The Times was right. Unfortunately, some two and one half hours and eighteen scenes later, nothing else in the play had risen to the height of that exquisite moment.

Second, I believe the play had a spiritual shortcoming in that it put too much emphasis on trying to see God, rather than on seeing purpose in the world He had made. Of the multitudes in *The Eternal Road,* the only individual who actually did see God was one of the children, a 12-year-old boy (played by Sidney Lumet, now a leading film director). This lad, who sees the Creator, is supposedly permitted this privilege because as a child, he is still unsophisticated and pure in heart. While this may be a viable premise, it did not capture the imagination of the audience. I think, perhaps, the triumph of his insight was only an accident of his youth. The boy's reward in being allowed to see God was not really a victory over tribulation, as it would have been for any of the adults in the play. The fault lay in the playwriting.

However, it is interesting to note that almost 40 years later another play, which also depicted the tragedy of the eternal road of Jewish persecution, did become a smash hit on Broadway, and an even greater success as a film. But this production, using a relatively humble story and setting, was able to accomplish what Max Reinhardt, with his panoramic spectacle of Old Testament history, had been unable to do. *Fiddler on the Roof* was the tale of one man, his family and his village. Yet through this warm, compassionate drama the tragedy of the entire Jewish people came to life. The reality and simplicity of communication with God was never more appealingly presented than in the conversation which the farmer, Tevya, (played so sensitively in the film by Israeli actor Topol), has with his Creator as he moves with his milk cart down a country road, debating with God on the verities of heavenly favors. It was beautiful and it was epic.

Holy Scriptures make the point that only when we become as children will we be able to enter the Kingdom of Heaven. Obviously that analogy is intended to point out the purity of heart with which a child looks at the world. I would contend, however, that only an adult heart, one that has experienced the pain, the compromise and the wonder of overcoming the obstacles of this world, is in an adequate position of understanding to appreciate Almighty God's purpose in Creation. And only when we comprehend that purpose can heaven of any kind, in this world or the next, have meaning for us, or be worth directing our efforts to attain.

By this time in my continuing discourse with God, though I felt I was beginning to unravel the enigma of Divine purpose in this world, I still felt no such insight into life-after-death, or whatever it might be that would climax this life. Not that I gave it too much thought at the time, for when one is young and in love the question of other worlds seems often too remote to ponder. And, as so often happens, one soon discovers that love has its own set of earthly heavens—and hells—which demand attention right here and now. Certainly the evaluation and any relation of either to Divine purpose is best done in retrospect, which only time and distance can provide—like looking back from the cool height of 78 years to the hot plains of 31.

Affairs of the heart had not been my long suit, though I had a fair share. But, because I hated city life, I spent most of my free time trying to get away from it—on weekends, when most young men of my age were dating, I was off hiking or bicycling in the country. As a result, my mooncalf days were brief and of small consequence. And after we purchased the farm in 1928, I would still commute to New York City, as theatrical work called me, but my heart was revelling in the chance to work the soil and to build upon the land. I sent away to our N.Y. State Agricultural Experiment Station for dozens of pamphlets. I would read them in the city and apply them on the farm. An illustration of this overlap occurred early in 1930.

I was rehearsing in the new George Gershwin Musical *Girl Crazy,* a story about a dude ranch, in which I did a brief rope-spinning number. As with all rehearsals there are long periods of waiting while other scenes than your own are being set. On one such occasion I was sitting on the floor at the rear of the stage, reading my ag bulletins. One of the chorus girls, a lovely charmer whom I was rather taken with, came over to ask me, "What on earth are you reading that is so engrossing?" I showed her the pamphlet, "Home Butchering on the Farm." She let out a squeal and backed away from me. Somehow my lifestyle did not encourage romance.

I mention these things only because it is impossible for me to write about spiritual values without including the background of daily experiences, for these give them meaning. There are two sides to the coin of life, and neither can exist apart from the other. This, I believe, is the prime reason why total separation of church and state are truly impossible. Religious and moral values cannot exist without pragmatic experiences upon which to mold them.

I don't recall any special philosophic insights resulting from my year's run with *Girl Crazy*, except that in the matter of moral values I had to admire the courage of Willie Howard, the show's comedian. During rehearsals Willie was asked to include some off-color lines in his performance. Willie refused, saying that it was a sad day when comedy was reduced to depending on the bathroom or the gutter for laughs. It was not in good taste, it indicated lack of talent on the part of the show's writers, and he would have no part of it. Today, one could wish that more leading performers, writers, and theatrical producers had Willie Howard's perception that, without good taste in the theatre, the end product of their profession becomes ugly, shabby, and its future dismal indeed.

In *Girl Crazy* Willie Howard was featured along with two talented young ladies who were making their first bid for stardom—Ginger Rogers and Ethel Merman. Ginger I knew best, because several afternoons a week throughout the long run of the show she would come down to the theatre to practice dance steps. I would be there, too, because I worked out daily with my lariats to keep in shape for my rope spinning number in the show. Ropes, like dancing feet, require a lot of practice. Ginger practiced very hard, indeed, and I was delighted to watch her, in the years that followed, make the success her diligent efforts so richly deserved.

Incidentally, in the matter of practice, I realize now that it was lack of practice at paying attention to the girls which made so many of my own stage performances seem inadequate during those first five summers of our Starlight Theatre. I had the opportunity, then, to play a number of excellent parts, including Capt. Bluntschlie in Shaw's *Arms and the Man,* and Browning in *The Barretts of Wimpole Street.* My performances drew considerable attention, but nothing ever really came of the possibilities. I'm convinced now it was because my performances lacked emotional depth—which was surely a reflection of the hiatus in my personal life, so that when in 1938 I really fell deeply in love for the first time, I handled it rather badly. The girl was a lovely ingenue in our stock company. Mother, as director, thought the young lady had a promising future as an actress, and that marriage would spoil her chances. So we fought about it.

Actually my dear mother, who was a theatrical genius, really, had two troublesome quirks in her character which, up until that time, I had not fully understood or had occasion to rationalize. Mother had a very strong "silver-cord" complex, which made it difficult for her to see any of her children leave the home nest. In addition to this well-known psychological phobia, Mother truly believed that marriage clipped an artist's wings. Thus she vigorously opposed marriage for every one of her children. Already, my two middle brothers had run afoul of that traumatic influence and had severed their family contacts because of it.

Now it was my turn. It was not an easy transition to make. Ours had been a more than usually close family.

There was great love between us and a mutual respect for each other's talents and predilections. This made it all the harder when separation resulted because of affairs of the heart. For here, as far as Mother was concerned, was the parting of the ways. If you got married, you left the family circle. For good. There was no middle ground, no happy keeping-in-contact while leading separate lives, as with most normal families.

The net result, in my case, was a three-way split. That summer my fiancee, disconsolate over the situation, left New York and sailed for Australia with a road-show company of Clare Booth Luce's *The Women*. I left home and the family business enterprise, and with letters of introduction in my pocket from our good friend Lowell Thomas, headed for California and the film capital in Hollywood. The car I drove belonged to my fiancee who had left it in my care along with her Dalmatian dog, Suzzie. Since I believed then that I would never return to the East Coast again, I decided to take both the car and the dog with me and deliver them to her in California when her ship returned from Australia.

CHAPTER III

My Years Alone:

Go West Young Man

*A*s I drove west, for the first time in my life completely alone, free to make decisions, to plan and live for myself only, I began once more to analyze life's purpose, searching for that place where I might fit in with what I now believed to be God's eternally evolving universe. Earlier that year I had been Lowell Thomas' dinner guest at the Adventurer's Club in New York City, where he graciously introduced me as a young man whom they would surely hear more from in the future. Lowell, an extensive traveler, whose journeys had penetrated some of the earth's most out-of-the way places, understood my own penchant for wilderness hiking and I rather imagine he expected me to challenge the firmament in same dramatic way. I know I was thinking of that while I was driving to California that fall of 1938.

Crossing the Mississippi, following the sun across the broad states of Kansas, Oklahoma and Texas, I caught up with, and drove through, several of the violent dust storms then plaguing those prairie lands. For mile after mile I might see no one, nor pass another car. No smooth, efficient interstate highways in those days—they hadn't even been thought of yet. But limitless views of the horizon, interrupted by a total "no-view" while going through swirling dust storms, evoked an atmosphere singularly conducive to communication with one's Creator. Once more I launched into debates:

"Lowell expects me to challenge the frontiers of the world, Lord. Now You know how much I've always wanted to wrestle with the forces of nature beyond the outskirts of civilization. But those frontiers are really all gone. Where can I find that challenge now?"

"That depends on your understanding of what constitutes a challenge or a frontier." As usual God was forcing me to research my own question.

"I suppose, Lord, in its broadest sense, frontier is the outer edge of anything you can name?"

"Yes, my son, there are frontiers to everything—city life, farming, medicine, engineering, politics, science. There have to be. You learned that when you discovered that the Universe is still evolving."

"Yes, of course, Lord." That was one of the things I'd learned about arguing with God. He always spoke from the basis of logic. "And I suppose, Lord, there's a frontier to philosophy and religion, too?"

"One of the most dangerous, my son. You're probing along the edge of that one right now."

"I see. And You're telling me, Lord, that I can find challenge there, or really in any area where I may choose to place my efforts?"

"You're telling yourself. You're discovering answers because you're taking time to examine this world where I've set you down—and, deep in your heart, to wonder."

"So then, Lord, challenge can be a dare, a summons—or an invitation?"

"*Certainly. It depends on any specific situation, and how you rise to meet it. Like now.*" Again God was turning the question back on me.

I did not reply at once. Trying to marshal my thoughts I scanned the countryside as my car rolled westward. Then, on the grassy plains I saw a herd of cattle—Herefords, I noted, their familiar red-brown hides mottled with white patches, lending a pleasing effect to the landscape. I figured they were mostly heifers, due for calving in the spring. Yet on the edge of the herd I saw two young ones suckling their mothers. Fall calves, I judged, probably born in August, the result of last year's late pasture breeding, not the most desirable time from the stockman's viewpoint, for increasing one's herd. But Nature moves inexorably to populate the earth, regardless of man-made schedules. However, if grazing remained plentiful until snows fall, the three-month's old calves should winter well enough on the open range, their built-in urge for self-preservation accepting the eternal challenge of birth— the daily struggle to feed the body.

As my car sped onward the cattle dropped away in my rear view mirror, but the fleeting thought about their need to contend every day of their lives for food rode on with me, like a hitch-hiker picked up out of nowhere, a strange companion prying into my thoughts, provoking answers.

The eternal challenge of birth—the phrase stayed with me, teasing my brain. Man's daily struggle to feed his body—was that not an invitation, or a supreme dare, that God places before every living creature? Then followed this thought:

> If such a challenge to prevail over obstacles is the crucial determinant for our life's beginning and its daily continuation on this planet, may it not also be an integral part of our purpose here?

"Yes, Lord," I picked up the dialogue again, "I believe that's the only coherent way to look at it. Thus, from such a perspective, the challenge to overcome has to be in everything that life presents—a Divine gauntlet flung to us—to be picked up or ignored. And because You, Lord, have given us free will the choice is completely ours, isn't it? What tremendous and awesome opportunities that insight offers us. By rising to challenges we can move forward the development of Your eternally evolving universe—or we can pass them by. But, if we avoid the issues of this world, where You, Lord, have placed us, what possible good can we be to You in whatever other worlds may follow? The logic is inescapable."

The miles were adding up on my odometer. Already I'd gone many, many hundreds of miles since leaving New York. Now I was out in the Texas panhandle driving through another dust storm, the fine particles sifting through the edge of the car's closed windows, adding an unpleasant, gritty flavor to the doughnuts I was munching as I rode along. It made me think of the multitudes of Americans (farmers and small town folks) who were displaced by these same dust storms. Courageously they had migrated away from the drought-tortured areas to create new lives elsewhere, even as their ancestors, moving west in covered wagons, had come out here originally, battling Indians, privation and inhospitable nature to pioneer what was then the frontier of a great new nation. Now they were moving on again, daring the unknown.

What was it in people that responded so vigorously to crisis? Why does it seem that people cooperate more readily, with more genuine brotherhood, under the stress of war or calamity? Even the least observant citizen can't help noticing how people will pull together more unselfishly when a local crisis hits a community, than they will in unruffled times of peace and tranquillity? Fire, flood, famine, war or disease. They stir people to extend themselves. That day, as I swallowed my gritty doughnuts, I knew I was discovering a basic truth about man—God had created us with an ingrained drive to rise above the difficult. Just as man responds to the perpetual daily challenge to feed the hunger of his body, so his spirit responds to the challenge to overcome obstacles. Was it God's provision for creating eternal evolution in the universe? And toward what purpose?

When I arrived in California a few days later, I found some formidable obstacles that soon put my new philosophical discoveries to the test.

Once in Hollywood I proceeded to use my letters of introduction from Lowell. They got me in to see several prominent executives at Twentieth Century Fox, Columbia and Universal. The gentlemen were gracious and would have helped me to gain immediate work in the industry, had I not made a stupid decision before calling on them at the studios. My years on Broadway and in our summer theatre had left me with little desire to pursue an acting career. Yet, during our summer stock seasons the tasks of producing, directing and set building had developed in me latent skills which I could have employed to real advantage in film making. But,

when those executives asked me what I wished to do in
the industry, I told them I wanted to write! To which
they replied, "Fine. Go home and write something exciting, then bring it to us."

So, day after day, at my one-room garage apartment
in the hills just above Hollywood and Vine streets, I sat
myself down before the table and tried to write. But it
did not come easily. Long hours of desk work irritated
me. One afternoon I pushed aside the penciled pages
(I've never been able to create on a typewriter) and
looked out the window for a long while. Then I burst
out laughing at myself. Here I was laboring at a desk—
the very sort of occupation from which I had so vio-
lently shied away those many years ago when I first
reached New York. Now I had voluntarily trapped myself into doing what I intensely disliked, pushing a pen
across paper. Why had I told the studios I wanted to
write?

I didn't care a damn about being a writer. I wanted
to be active, on my feet, using my brains and my
hands. Yet, I had written. Why? I wrote several plays
and some radio dramas. They had been produced and
received favorable response. But why had I undertaken
to write them in the first place?

That afternoon in my Hollywood Hills apartment I
tried to analyze the reason, and discovered that I had
begun writing in answer to a specific challenge. Our
summer theatre needed certain kinds of plays, and we
had used up all the available scripts of such types, so,
on the spur of the moment, I volunteered. I sat down
and wrote two plays to fill that need. The next season,
my brother Ted, searching out wider fields of publicity

for our shows, developed a deal with Radio Station WTIC at Hartford, Connecticut, to put on a weekly radio drama for them each Sunday which would use some of the name actors currently playing at our Starlight Theatre. "Fine," they replied, "but where would the dramas come from?" Said Ted, "Oh, my brother Starr will write them."

And so I did, though finding time and quiet for creative writing was something of a problem. My days were already crowded with rehearsing parts and building scenery for the next week's play, while performing each evening in the current drama and, in between, going up to the farm, twice daily, to milk our family cow. But after the show, when everyone else had gone to bed, I'd take my clipboard and go up onto the semi-dark stage. Sitting there, gazing up at the high, arching barn rafters I'd somehow pull ideas and characters out of the shadows. Thus each week, a new radio drama was born.

But now in Los Angeles without a special need to fill, my mind dawdled, and physical impatience made it difficult to follow the writer's code which says: Writing success depends upon the application of the seat of the pants to the seat of the chair. I knew, at this rate, it would be a long time before my reluctant efforts produced any monetary returns from the studios, and I had to have an income.

My pride (shades of Cyrano!) would not let me tell the studios that now I didn't want to write, so I simply went out and got myself a job as night manager with a well-known restaurant chain. This left my mornings free for occasional visits to the studios and to continue some writing. Somehow, after my conversation with God about overcoming obstacles, I felt I couldn't quit altogether. Besides, I didn't want to let Lowell down.

In the next three years I wrote two film scripts (none were accepted) and composed another radio drama series for a station back East. But, while my writing lagged, my restaurant job flourished. It kept me very active, continually on my feet. I enjoyed that and the daily contact with people. Then the restaurant owners offered me the management of a new, deluxe dining establishment which they were building. This meant I would have to give up any sideline efforts, like my desultory writing, and devote full time to the restaurant work. When I hesitated to accept, the management upped the monetary inducement to a share of the profits. The new restaurant was scheduled to open in May and it was now April of 1941. It was just too good an opportunity to pass up, so I agreed.

But something was happening, thousands of miles away, which would prevent my ever seeing that bright, new building and a promising new career. On the twenty-third of April, 1941, I was drafted into the United States Army.

CHAPTER IV

The War Years:

*Immortality, Violent Death,
And Prayers For Peace*

𝕴n that spring of 1941, the German blitzkrieg of
Europe had reached the Channel. England was
being bombed night and day. The United States
Congress, sensing our nation's possible involvement,
had begun to call up American citizens for a one year
period of military training. The first call had been
made in October of 1940; the second draft came in the
spring of '41 and my name was on the list. Though I
was already 35 at the time, I was still unmarried and,
perhaps, enhanced by my reputation for hiking and
camping, I was a natural candidate for soldiering.
On April 23, 1941, I was sworn into the Army and
sent to join the 7th Infantry Division at Fort Ord, California.

Management of the restaurant chain, expecting I
would be away for only a one-year training tour, said
"Go ahead. We'll get the new house opened, the bugs
worked out of operations, and hold it for you to take
over when the year is up."

Alas, for the best laid plans of mice and men, it was almost seven years before I came off active duty and could return to civilian pursuits. By that time the world was not the same—I had risen from private to major, trained thousands of new lieutenants at Fort Benning, married a provocative, red-headed gypsy, fought through France and Germany as a rifle company commander and served in the occupation of Austria as a staff intelligence officer, during which time my wife joined me overseas. When we returned to the States in late 1947, I had changed my whole outlook on what I might do with my life. But contrary to a popular belief which holds that time spent in military service is time lost out of one's life, I had found that for me it was a period of surprising development in skills as well as the nature of my inner being, both of which would move my life forward in directions I had never dreamed of before.

The world at war is a planet exposed to the fury of a titanic thunder storm. Troops in the field experience the full lash of the violence—there is nothing between them and their Maker except their own resourcefulness. Installations and personnel (military or civilian), when housed in buildings, are surrounded by the seemingly protective walls of man's creation, momentarily secure from the stinging rain, though not the searing lightning, the shaking thunder nor the tearing-apart visited upon all structures and all living creatures by the stupendous force of cyclonic winds. A poet, watching how dead branches are ripped from trees in a tempest, observed that "a tree cleanses itself in a storm." Now, I wondered, could the storm of war do the same for civilization?

For my own self I discovered that, in the same manner that a storm's lightning splits the sky asunder, so did the flashes of war's onslaught illuminate for me hidden, interior vistas of God's universe. Some of those vivid insights have remained with me through all the forty years since.

I recall one such experience while training at Fort Ord, California, in the tense days before Pearl Harbor. I had been attending church service at the Rec Hall and later that night wrote down the following observation:

"Why did Private Stone go to church service this morning? Certainly not to look at the rafters of the Rec Hall; he sees them every day. Certainly not to hear the cliche phrases as the chaplain leads the congregation through the time-worn ritual. Yet I do know that Stone went there for a purpose because as I stood beside the flying crosses that waved from guidon standards in front of the building, Stone passed me, and I saw that certain questing look in his eyes.

"I had seen that look before once, in a smoky barroom, on an old woman selling flowers. She stopped in front of me as I lit my pipe. By the flare of the match I caught her off guard and surprised that look in her eyes. She left a flower by my glass on the bar and hurried away. Again, late one afternoon at Ord, I had strolled to the top of a low hill overlooking the ocean. I had been whistling, but now I stopped and listened—it seemed the melody still hung, suspended in air, while the voice of eons past rolled up from the crest of the pounding surf below. A gull wheeled over my head, the sharp sound of its pinons like a faint whisper from another world. Then the bird disappeared into the horizon—as though pressing to catch up with the vanishing sun.

"I don't know how long I stood there, caught in the spell of recorded music from an unfinished symphony playing out its chords and harmonies of centuries past and still to come. The never-ending deliberations with my Creator surfaced again. What, I wondered now, with the shadows of war growing darker, would be my own part in this ongoing divine composition? Where was I to play my brief interlude in the impending orchestral arrangement which would record this present phase of man's struggles toward a better world? For the first time I felt a desire to see the face of God, the countenance of the great Maestro. I had a feeling that if I could but catch His eyes, He, with a wave of His baton, would place me where I belonged.

The first star blinked on while the afterglow of twilight still held the sky alight. I sighed and turned to go, then realized that I was not alone. The figure of a young boy stood a few feet behind me, legs wide apart, hands in pockets, his face looking out to sea. Unconsciously, the lad was standing even as I had been—and that same look was in his eyes. His gaze held mine and I knew that the question his eyes asked was the same that trouble my own soul—where does one make contact with God?

"Listen," he said, and we both held our breath. High above the ceaseless, rolling surf there hovered a thin unearthly silence, like the void that follows the last note of a violin, empty yet pregnant with the secret of life. For one wild, brief moment I felt that I might get lost in that void—then my fear shrank before the steady gaze of the youth, and I smiled. The lad smiled back, such a warm, friendly grin. And, in that instant, as though a curtain had been raised behind the shutter of those eyes, I saw a light shine forth and I knew I looked upon the hidden face of the Great Maestro. Such a simple answer—it is deep within the eyes of another human being that our own eyes may brush, momentarily, the countenance of God.

"The spell of that discovery was still fresh in my mind this morning as I watched Private Stone enter the Rec Hall. I followed, and from the back of the auditorium saw the good chaplain talking to those before him. But his efforts fell, like spent arrows about their feet, wasted, for his eyes never met those in the faces before him. Never once did he let the magic of smiling eyes contact, for an instant, the Divinity within each man.

"I left the service full of sorrow for Private Stone, but even more for the Army chaplain who, I felt, had so failed to meet the need of men preparing for combat. I am afraid my thoughts were most uncharitable toward this man who had dedicated his life to bringing men closer to God. And that would have been the end of another brief episode in my spiritual pilgrim's progress, except for a scrap of information that reached me sometime later and which made me ashamed that I had been so harsh in my judgment of a humble and fine man: it seems the chaplain had, previous to his present military assignment, been stationed for a very long time as the warden of souls in a mental hospital—and who shall say that his transfixed gaze, above the heads of men, had not been so developed while ministering to those unfortunate people whose inner being knows not how to remain within the confines of a normal body—but whose souls must wander, perchance in space, just a little ways off.

"For the next few days I went about my duties in a much humbler frame of mind, determined not to let my personal bias ever again trip me into prejudging my comrades." Yes, that's how I had written it down.

The first weeks of basic training were, for me, no more than a review of what I had been doing for years: rolling a watertight pack, using a compass, care of the feet on the march, camp sanitation and, of course, rifle practice. Later, assigned as assistant driver on an army 6 × 6 truck, I learned about "double clutching" (to keep vehicles rolling through sand or mud) and how to drive in convoy, cross-country at night, with only the vehicle's cat's-eye black-out lights to tell the position of the

truck ahead of me, which half of the time was so hidden in swirling dust that you could catch only fleeting
glimpses of those dark-blue one-inch spots. I tell you
that's a wild adventure. Many months later, as our
near-victorious troops, loaded on tanks and trucks,
rolled through the black night toward Munich and the
infamous death camp at Dachau, I would have a hair
raising experience with too many blackout lights, and
then, suddenly, none at all. But more of that later.

There is a statement in Scripture that God does not
allow more trouble to come upon us than the strength
of our shoulders can bear, and I have found this to be
true. I have discovered that the Lord is constantly preparing us to handle such burdens by guiding us into
experiences which, if our hearts are perceptive, do
sharpen our awareness of God's presence, strengthen
our emotions, and thereby build up our spiritual resources against the future demands of crisis. One such
experience came my way only a few weeks before
Pearl Harbor. It came about while on furlough at the
end of summer maneuvers. But first a word about
those exercises.

Training maneuvers meant weeks of mock battles,
digging and crawling in the dust and sand of the scrub-
covered hills at Camp Roberts, some miles inland from
William Randolph Hearst's castle, which overlooks the
Pacific Ocean at San Simeon. I soon learned that the
average enlisted soldier is frequently confused about
where he is at any given moment and about what his
presence is accomplishing at that particular spot, anyway.

On this maneuver I was as much in the dark as the rest of the men of our company. But on the third day an enterprising civilian lad from a nearby town came through our position selling newspapers. The headline article gave a detailed account of our "Seventh Infantry Division's War Games." In addition to identifying units and their mission, the paper also showed a sketch map of the area. The men of our service company gathered around the paper as we tried to locate ourselves on the maps. Once that was accomplished every man wanted a copy of the article but the newsboy had already left the area. I went to our first sergeant. Louie Rhettman had been a captain in WWI, and afterward joined the Regular Army as a first sergeant. He was a rugged individual who knew combat so I asked him:

"Sergeant, would it compromise our operations if I made tracing copies of this newspaper map for the men? I think they'll have more interest in the maneuvers if they can readily locate where they are."

"Sure, go ahead," replied Rhettman, "only don't mark our position in case one of the sketches falls into enemy hands. Incidentally, did you stop to think, maybe that newsboy could have been an informer?"

"Hey, Sergeant, I never thought of that. Maybe I shouldn't make the copies?"

"No, go ahead, make them. Blank maps can't hurt. But just remember, if you want to stay alive in wartime, it pays to be suspicious of everybody and everything. Americans tend to be too trusting. You'll find that out when you get overseas."

I made the overlays, gave them to the men and passed on the first sergeant's advice. I would remember it later, in

France, when civilian refugees were streaming through our positions in advance of the German assault.

One night, some weeks later, our maneuvers had taken us to the evergreen forests of Fort Lewis, Washington. As ammunition sergeant, my assignment kept me scrambling from one end to the other of our regiment's assigned combat area relaying orders for rifle, machine gun and mortar rounds. It was raining and the night was pitch black as I found my way to the rear echelon supply area. With the aid of my flashlight's tiny one-inch strip of blue light, I located the "ammo dump" sign on the dark side of a large tent which blocked my way through the even darker forest. I raised the flap and slipped inside. A shaded kerosene lantern cast more shadows than light. As soon as I grew accustomed to the eerie shadows I saw that a soldier was standing behind an improvised table made of ammo boxes. But under the helmet I could discern only a pair of eyes in the black space where a face should have been.

"I'm Sergeant Jones," I said. "I have orders for ammo for the 53d Regiment."

"Sergeant Jones welcomes Sergeant Jones!" said a voice from under the helmet. Then, as though a small spotlight had been turned on the invisible head, a gleaming row of white teeth flashed in the black space below the eyes. Sergeant Jones had a smile as bright as his visage was black. I gave him the slip of paper on which were marked the amounts of ammunition our units needed. Sgt. Jones scribbled more figures on another piece of paper and handed it back to me.

"Sgt. Jones delivers to Sgt. Jones three thousand rounds." He chuckled and his face lit up with another smile. "Sounds stupid, doesn't it, carrying pieces of paper around the country in the dark as though they were real bullets?"

"That's what simulated combat is all about." I replied.

"What good does it do? If this was real combat..."

"I'd still have to find my way to you in the dark." I said, "And you'd have to account for our ammo needs in order to keep your own supply moving up."

"O.K. Sarge, I see. I see." Again that flashing smile. "And should I simulate helping you load those 3,000 rounds on your empty truck now?"

"Thanks, no, Sergeant. But you've got a good sense of humor. Hang on to it. Incidentally, my truck in not empty. There's five and a half cases of live ammo in it right now."

"Live? .30-caliber stuff or mortar shells?"

"Neither, just 22s."

"Twenty twos? For what? The army going squirrel hunting?"

"No, for target practice on the range. They're just as accurate and a lot less expensive for training. Government has to save money, you know."

"How about letting me have a few boxes, Sergeant? I think I saw some rabbits today."

"Sorry, Sergeant, can't do it. I have to account for every last round with a written report each day. Count them each night before I turn in."

With that I pocketed my paper ammunition supply and raising the tent flap, went out again into the dark and the rain. Sgt. Jones followed and stood beside me as I paused to get my bearings.

"That your ammo truck down there to the side of the road?"

"It could be, for I left it down there, somewhere, though I can't see it myself now. How can you?"

"No trouble at all," replied the ammo dump soldier. "I'm at

home in all shades of darkness. Good luck, Sergeant."
"Same to you, Sgt. Jones." I replied as I walked away.

When I reached my truck I looked back toward where I had left the good-humored sergeant. I could see nothing at all. Then, for a fleeting instant, a sliver of pale yellow appeared in the opaque distance and I knew Sgt. Jones with his light-hearted, pearly bright smile was re-entering the tent. I would like to have given him some of those rounds. Maybe I took my duties too seriously. But, anyway, the seriousness produced a momentary touch of humor a few months later on the very day Pearl Harbor was bombed.

Across the country, on that fateful Sunday, the entire military machine was put on full alert. In less than an hour, all units of our 53d Infantry Regiment had stripped camp, loaded men and equipment on trucks and were moving out of Fort Ord assigned to protect the Union Pacific Railroad, our West Coast's vital link with the industrial heartland.

As I climbed aboard the last S-4 supply truck, already filled with soldiers armed with the newly issued M-1 rifles, one of the men pointed to the several boxes of my carefully counted .22-caliber rounds on the floor of the truck.

"Hey Sarge," he said scornfully, "what are we going to do with your precious 22s? This is real war now."

"Don't worry about those bee-stingers," put in one of the other men. "The sarge will issue each man a handful, we'll throw them into our mouths and spit them out at the enemy!"

The men laughed and the truck convoy moved out, with several vehicles towing behind them our only anti-tank guns, mock training weapons made from a pole on an axle and two wheels, draped with a camouflage net. It seems that our American army, ever since Revolutionary War days, has always, somehow, moved out to fight the enemy traditionally short of the necessary arms. But one weapon we did have in bountiful supply, and it carried us to victory time and again—the sense of humor of the American soldier.

So, the battle was joined, I thought to myself as our regimental convoy rolled north toward our designated first rendezvous point, the Stockton Fairgrounds. This was the real thing, at last. I looked at the faces of the men around me in the jostling truck—the young men eager, the older ones more thoughtful—a mix of draftees and regular army, the manpower of a peaceful nation about to commit their lives in a furious struggle to reach a higher plateau of universal respect for human rights. Except for the rifles and uniforms they might have been an elevator full of average Americans on their way to work in any city that ominous Sunday, the 7th of December, 1941.

As the trucks rolled on, I looked out the back at the pleasant California landscape, so calm and peaceful on either side of the road. A few miles off to the right would be the Pacific Ocean where we now knew the Japanese war machine was marshaling against our shores. And, off to the left, eastward, the Sierras, whose rocky spine divides California from Nevada and Arizona. I sensed her snow-topped ranges watching in serenity the sudden activity of Americans (ever a resourceful people in the face of crisis) moving purposefully to meet this new emergency which could mean sudden or lingering death for many of us. I glanced again at my fellow soldiers in the truck. How many of them, I wondered, were now thinking about that possible termination of their lives?

For myself, I had faced up to that question only a few weeks earlier in those same Sierra mountains. It was at the conclusion of summer maneuvers when all soldiers were given two weeks leave. While most men went home to visit their families I packed a haversack and headed eastward for the magnificent rock masses of Yosemite National Park. Somehow I sensed that this short respite, in the growing turmoil that was spreading over the globe, might well be a last intermission before the Horsemen of the Apocalypse would sweep many of us before them into final Judgment. I had a yearning to regain, once again, the rapport with my Creator which I had first discovered those many years ago in the Michigan forest.

Since draftees were not permitted to retain civilian clothes in barracks I had only my wool uniform to move in. But this was a good outfit for hiking. From the company supply sergeant I drew a compass, regulation pack, blanket, shelter half, mess kit and canteen. Thus equipped, I was ready for the miles ahead. As it turned out I actually hiked 265 miles in the eleven days, climbing from 3,985 feet on the Yosemite Valley floor to over 11,000 feet at the pass between Mt. Lyell and Isberg Peak. The following are extracts from the journal I kept of that trip:

"**Wednesday, September 24:** I reached Yosemite by bus. At the General Store I purchased some twenty pounds of food and from the park rangers secured a contour map, over which we traced the route I planned to take. Snow comes early in the high Sierra country, they explained to me, and since the summer season was over, there would be no people on the remote trails I would be following, so they would notify the other ranger stations to be on the lookout for a lone soldier. They also volunteered to transport half of my food supplies to the station at Tuolmone Meadows, where I could pick them up when I reached that half-way point on my trek...

"The next morning I was off, up the trail, reaching Glacier Point in the early afternoon, 3,214 feet above the valley floor. From here the view was breathtaking—Yosemite Falls, Half Dome and El Capitan before me, with range after range of snowy peaks beyond. I studied the ranges carefully, trying to pick out landmarks to those mountain passes through which I must climb. Somewhere out there, beyond Mt. Lyell, I knew, was the trail I sought. Somewhere out there, I hoped, I would again make contact with the Creator of this magnificent universe...I hiked on.

Four o'clock: Passing Taft Point which overlooks the westward view of Yosemite—a lone hawk and myself the only spectators...then, away from the canyon's rim, back into the deep forest and across Perigoy Meadows. A herd of mustangs, turned out for winter pasture, galloped away at sight of me, then turned to follow inquisitively as, with failing daylight at my back, I entered an even darker wood along Alder Creek. Hiked for an hour through shadowy lanes, with an occasional glimpse of the new quarter moon above the trees. Camped that night between two huge stones where the reflecting heat from my cook fire made cozy sleeping and dispelled the heavy frost that spread beyond the reach of its warm fingers...

For the next two days I hiked ever higher and deeper, into the fastness of these majestic mountains. On the third day I wrote in my journal:

"John Muir may have been the first to explore and record their beauty but, for myself, coming to them from the turmoiled canyons of skyscraper New York and the harlequin unreality of our film capital, I felt I was in a far better position to appreciate their grandeur and tranquility. The joy of traveling these trails is heightened by being alone with only the birds or squirrels to scold as the sound of my footfalls disturbs the solitude...

"Sometimes, when the going was particularly steep or rough, I would be out of breath and feel I must rest before going another step. But my feet ignored the demands of the rest of my body and, with a will of their own, learned through long years of self discipline, they kept on and on, one foot following the other steadily, forward—ever forward—till I began to wonder at this detachment of one part of my body from the voluntary will which was supposed to control it. It is quite a lofty sensation to discover you have trained a body which carries on for you in spite of yourself...

Sept. 24th, Four o'clock: I reached the crest of Fernandez Pass, (elevation 11,175 feet), southern boundary line between Yosemite Park and the Sierra National Forest, beyond whose distant ranges rose the misty head of Mount Whitney, highest in the continental United States. On this side of the pass were small, blue flowers growing among the rocks. On the other side before me stretched a field of perpetual snow. I rested my pack upon the white surface and gazed eastward spellbound at serried ranks of snow-capped peaks glistening in the westering sun. Some of my Indian ancestors had referred to these as corridors in the lodge of the great Kigee Manitou, and they had built no churches to physically contain the person of their Creator. In their simplicity they seem to have recognized the illimitability of God, and they were content to acknowledge His presence in the handiwork of His universe.

In the rarefied mountain atmosphere one can see very clearly—for great distances. Standing there, alone, upon the heights I looked long across the centuries-old upthrust, and as I did so I sensed that the immovable, craggy mass was staring back at me. Staring at this bit of human flesh, (life span but a moment) who in only a few days had climbed to this notch in the rocks, here to command an overlook of the Sierra ranges, that magnificent body of atoms which had taken millions of years to reach its present position on the face of the planet, where now, together, we shared an instant of eternity.

I don't know how long I stood there in contemplation, but my gaze at last turned inward upon myself. Much that had before seemed always murky I saw for the first time clearly—even into the years ahead, and I whispered to myself:

"This moment I am alive as never before. This moment I am drinking in great draughts of stimulation from the Creator. Though by nightfall death might take me by surprise on the trail, I shall feel my life fulfilled. Though I might fall down a rocky ravine, even be struck by a bolt from one of the sudden lightning storms which are born out of the beauty of the clouds above these mountain ranges or, later, face the grim reaper on some distant battlefield, it will make small difference, for here, at this spot in time, silently, without speaking, I have achieved oneness with God. I have touched the sublime and can face all of the future unafraid.

"I picked up my pack and started on the down trail. After about a mile I struck timberline again, and a little further on, in a grove of tall tamarack trees, reached a stream, fed from the snow fields above. An ideal campsite.

"Collected wood, built a lean-to frame facing my fireplace, over which I stretched my shelter half. Short limbs of mountain hemlock for a bed upon which I spread my raincoat and blanket. As darkness fell so did the temperature. Put on the woolen drawers I had brought, plus an extra pair of wool socks. After a hot supper of rolled oats, raisins and tea, I turned in.

"Awoke once during the night. The fire was almost out. I reached over to throw on a log, then looked around puzzled—it was late, the moon had set, yet the grove in which I lay camped was quite light. Then I saw, between two giant pine trees that framed, like some tall cathedral window, such an expanse of glittering stars as I had never beheld before—I was literally bathed in starlight!

"I lay there studying the heavens, fascinated, recalling the calculations of astronomers and their statistical estimates of the extent of this glowing universe. The thousands, maybe millions, of stars I saw with the naked eye were mostly in our own galaxy, the Milky Way. They were the same stars my ancestors saw, and upon which they based much of their religious and philosophical thinking. Yet, today electronic telescopes have revealed other galaxies than our own, billions of them, each containing more billions of stars, planets, moons and asteroids, out beyond, occupying space at distances that may only be calculated in light years—distances which dazzle the average mind to contemplate, a universe stretching out into infinity.

"I sat up, my arms about my knees, my eyes reaching out to draw that glittering immensity into my consciousness, eager to relate the fascination of unknown worlds to the realities of the one I knew and was struggling to better understand...

Now, once more, my inquiring mind transposed thoughts into discussions with the Creator:

"Out there, God, surely you must have other planets, other globes, inhabited like ours?"

"Does that seem logical?" As always the Lord's replies forced me to use reason.

"Of course," I insisted. "It's the only plausible explanation for such gigantic proliferation. If You consider that humanity makes so much out of the resources available on only this one planet, then to have untold billions of similar globes without inhabitants would seem to be a colossal waste, serving no purpose."

"Do you insist on purpose for everything?"

"Surely. You taught me that, Lord. All I see and work with here on this earth of Yours serves some purpose—even that which we look upon as bad or worthless can be turned to use.

Yes," I said, literally throwing my words into the night sky above me, "Yes, I believe in purpose!"

Now did I imagine it, or did one star actually blink twice? Was the Creator smiling at my vehemence? But I was determined to pursue the matter:

"Listen, Lord," I continued, "those other worlds out there, haven't they been evolving through the centuries, as we now know our own planet earth has been unfolding? Are they inhabited by other creatures like ourselves? Maybe more intelligent? Or, perhaps, farther back in evolutionary stage than we are now? Is it possible that some are still without living creatures, having only just reached the level of mineral and atmospheric properties where they are prepared to receive pioneers to develop their special planetary potential? Is it not possible that humans, who have successfully met the challenges of planet earth, would be well qualified to carry out that next phase of universal evolution?"

Once again I seemed to hear God speaking, gently: *"Is it logical?"*

"I'm not sure yet," I replied. "But it's a tantalizing thought. Yes, I know, Lord, we've only just begun to lift ourselves into space with airplanes, and rockets are still in laboratory stage. But I feel certain we will eventually move into outer space. Our technological advances, even in this year of 1941, are moving at a startling speed..."

Speed, that one word stopped me. What speeds attainable by man can carry his body across the fantastic distances measured by light years? I glanced across the night sky above me trying to imagine a single star that might become the focus of mankind's outreach. Though such an intriguing prospect was at odds with reality, I could not dismiss the idea. I felt sure that, in spite of obviously insurmountable obstacles, some dauntless human beings would tackle the impossible. To me that was one of the exciting things about the privilege of free will with which God had endowed us: there is no limitation upon what man's mind can aspire to and accomplish. His brain is his energy muscle, his spirit the fuel upon which it runs. Mind and spirit—the phrase caught hold of me. Mind and spirit are words that also define man's soul, that imperishable per-sonablity that goes on after death phases out the body in which it has been developed. The soul goes on—but to where?

Again I scanned the star-spangled night sky above me. Out there, somewhere, so Christian philosophy had taught me, there exists a place called heaven, where all good souls are destined to go. But it is a vague location, an area of no discernable dimensions, function or purpose. Other than to sing praises to the Heavenly King (a viewpoint inherited from feudal times) nothing is suggested to occupy the multitudes whom God is reportedly gathering there to be with Him for all eternity. To me it has always sounded totally unreal. When church literature promises heaven as the place where struggle ceases, when church hymns extoll heaven as the place where "there will be no dawning and no sunset," I shudder, for I want no part of such a dull future.

My Indian ancestors visualized heaven as a happy hunting ground with clear streams and much game, where the perpetual search for food and water would continue, though in pleasanter circumstances. For myself I have come to the conclusion that only in mastering the challenges of life do we find genuine happiness. The daily struggle to feed the body; the skirmish to acquire knowledge; the sparring for recognition; tilting to gain friends: battling to build a career; striving to win and to hold love, these are the vital encounters of this world, which God's eternal evolution presents to me. It is in meeting them that I've gained satisfaction, comfort, delight, even ecstasy. These continuing victories have conditioned my body, mind and spirit to press on to ever higher levels of attainment. I would wish for no less in the next world—but where is, what is, the world to come?

From my timberline campsite, high in the peaks of Yosemite, my gaze continued sweeping the sparkling sky, my eye pushing out in earnest effort to penetrate infinity, my heart still contending with the Creator for answers:

"Surely, God, you understand the direction of my reasoning. Now help me, please, where is that world to come? Is it the traditional, unlocatable heaven of Christian theory?"

"Why not?"

"Because, Lord, it follows no sound logic. To me it offers no purpose worth pursuing. It is not realistic."

"Then in just what form do you visualize the next world might be?"

Once more the Lord was challenging me to answer my own questions. Once more I paused to reason, to analyze... then, in a flash of intuition I replied:

"Might not our next world, Lord, be those countless other planets out there in space, those billions of celestial bodies which are slowly evolving into habitable worlds, possible of being occupied? Would not the development of their planetary resources serve a real purpose in Your ongoing evolution of the universe? If earth's humans cannot reach them now, because of the body limitations of this life, might not our spirits, our soul, be able to conquer the limitless distances to find new purpose, new challenge out there in the realistic heavens that fill outer space, reaching into infinity? Doesn't that make sense, Lord?"

"Does it seem logical to you, my son?"

"I think it might, Lord. The idea only just now occurred to me. I'll have to give it some study. But it's a fascinating prospect—let me think about it."

I don't know how long this debate had gone on under that starry sky, but suddenly I was aware of the night air's chill. I shivered, and turned to find my campfire almost out. Raking the coals together I put on more logs, and as the sparks danced up to meet the constellations, I lay down again, turned over contentedly, and went back to sleep.

The remaining eight days of the hike saw enough magnificent scenery to fill my soul's hunger for beauty for years to come. Though I did not again confront the Creator I offered many flash prayers of thanks for the inspirational banquet that seemed, each mile, to offer fresh nourishment to my soul. But one small event occurred, on the next to last evening of my Yosemite hike which needs telling here. Coming down from the high peak trails I reached the valley floor in the late afternoon of Thursday, the second of October, to discover that a forest fire was raging at the southwest entrance to the park. I hurried to the scene and reported to the ranger in charge of the firefighters.

"What can I do to help?" I asked.

"Plenty," he answered with a welcoming smile. Then looking past my shoulder he added, "And where is the rest of your outfit?"

Realizing that my uniform led him to expect others, I apologized. "Sorry, there's only myself. I'm on furlough, been hiking up around Mt. Lyell and Tuolomne. Smelled your smoke above the Falls and hurried down."

"Glad to have you," the ranger replied, "Here..."

Then he gave me a hose nozzle and a crew of half a dozen other men to help haul several thousand feet of hose behind me. A high-powered pump, set in the Merced River a few feet away, whined into action, a hundred foot stream of water spouted from the nozzle in my hands and our team moved into the twilight. Clambering up the steep, rocky slope of El Portal, we directed our water cannon at the bases of trees still blazing from the ground fire that had swept the forest floor into hot, black ashes before us. It was hot, wet slippery work, as we moved up and down that smoky mountainside throughout the night. But even rough toil has its moments of reward. From time to time during the night we would watch while some giant tree, blazing on fire at the canyon's rim above us, would finally break loose and fall, like a monstrous Roman candle, dropping with a shower of sparks for two thousand feet down into the canyon.

At dawn the fire was under control and I was released to complete my journey. I found a spot under a tree and slept for most of the day. In the late afternoon, thanks to a generous auto lift from a friendly tourist, I returned to the place where, on the first day of my hike, I had been able to view the whole range of mountains into which I would hike. We drove to Glacier Point, some 3,000 feet above the valley floor. We got out of the car and walked to the guard railing at the edge of the cliff which overlooked the valley of Yosemite.

The entry in my journal, which recorded that return, has, in the light of later years, a gentle note of irony. I wrote:

> "In the fading light the sublime peaks seemed to be receding into a shroud of mystery that sent a chill of unreality down my spine. From Gale Peak, far to the south, my gaze swept across the mighty pinnacled ranges to Cathedral Pass in the north, and I felt an odd thrill as something inside me whispered—"you've been there, you've walked and seen, you know their secret."
>
> Just then the friendly tourist touched my arm, and in a hushed voice, such as one uses in church, said, "Look—the clouds on Mt. Lyell!"
>
> Even as the voice spoke, the round arc of light rose above the cloud bank—in a few minutes the full, complete, yellow moon was riding the sky—mistress of the whole enchanting world below. As though reading my thoughts, I was sure that the face of that golden lady smiled—yes, her mountains still held their secret.
>
> Unconsciously, almost, I raised my hand in silent salute, and turning, went down from that place with peace and inspiration renewed in my heart.

From the State Fairgrounds in Sacramento (popularly known as the Cow Palace) our regiment moved out to guard the Union Pacific Railroad. The U.P. tracks run from Marysville, California, eastward, over the Donner Pass, across the bleak, snow-covered Nevada desert, and on to the critical rail yards at Ogden, Utah. Quickly we stationed units of armed soldiers at every bridge or culvert, every crossing, signal block or siding along the 1,200 miles of track. Then we were ready for Japanese attack anywhere on the California-Oregon coast. The speed of the maneuver, plus the willing cooperation of the civilian population again highlights, for me, the alacrity with which man rises to meet crisis. As I watched other crises come up, and be overcome by us time after time during the four years of the war, a conviction grew within me that there was a vital spiritual principle at work here which was, somehow, related to God's purpose for us being on this planet. Finding its place in the pattern became an important part of my quest.

Our regimental supply was based in a large garage in Ogden, Utah, and that's where I ended up. In addition to requisitioning ammunition, I helped order and distribute carloads of winter underwear and uniforms to the troops. One day I was ordered to take a truckload of worn GI shoes and go from cobbler to cobbler in the city of Ogden arranging for each shop to undertake repairing as many pairs as possible. Some took 25 pairs; one shop tackled 250. As I went about the task I recalled reading of Napoleon's army's movements in the early 19th century and it occurred to me that my boot assignment, to keep our soldiers shod, was not unlike that of Napoleon's quartermaster, scouring the countryside for horses to keep his army mobile. Was this history repeating itself?

It was during those three wintry months in Utah that I made my first acquaintance with the Mormons, a most remarkable people. With true western hospitality, as soon as our troops arrived in Ogden, the Mormon churches of the city began putting on dances and other social events for our soldiers. Never one to turn away from a dance, I took in my share of twirling the ladies, eating donuts and drinking fruit punch.

From those first kindly introductions I was to make two lifelong friends, and through them learn, at first hand, about the unusual beliefs of these gracious people. Created in the middle of the 19th century, the Mormon Church is one of the few groups of devout Christians to have made significant advances in spiritual thought beyond that which existed at the time when the Roman Empire first challenged the teachings of Jesus of Nazareth.

Let me say at this point I did not, and have not, become a Mormon, though I have certainly been often, and most lovingly, invited to share their faith. But, as stated at the outset of this book, I feel impelled to share with my readers whatever elements of spiritual nourishment I have discovered, no matter where, in my life's journey through this moment of eternity.

While I have not been persuaded to accept the theological precepts of the Mormon's Church of Jesus Christ of Latter Day Saints, over the years I have observed that in the daily practice of their faith they seem to have found at least partial answers to two of the spiritual puzzles that have troubled me for so long, "Why am I here?" and "Why should the Bible's recording of man's reaching out to God have stopped that account almost two thousand years ago?"

The books of the Old Testament make a logical sequence, for over 5,000 years, of the Jewish people's struggle to communicate with the Source of Creation. Yet the books of the New Testament dwell solely upon the relatively short years of the coming, preaching, and death of Jesus of Nazareth. They record, in the years immediately following his passing, the theology that his apostles created out of Jesus' teachings. That doctrine, derived mostly from the Gospel of St. John, became the substance of early Christian religion. Thus, the practice of the Christian church today stands almost wholly upon the theological interpretations of some men who lived 2,000 years ago, men who had no way of knowing how far beyond their age of thinking, both in technological and psychological evolutions, human life on this earth would advance. As a consequence, it seems to me our 20th century Christian philosophy is severely handicapped, offering scant logic to explain God's purpose for our lives, and too often failing sadly to make the church's teachings seem relevant to our world of today.

I want to explain, at this juncture, that when I critique certain elements of our Christian theology I mean no disrespect for the faith itself, or of the devout followers of Christendom's many denominations. It is only that I believe creeds and theologies need to progress. They should not stand still in time while the universe moves on. Each epoch of God's creation brings fresh insights, new possibilities and new challenges— theologically as well as materially. What I set down here are only my own attempts to meet those challenges as I have found them revealed to me in my own search for spiritual nourishment. For I believe that all creeds and theologies are important, and each serves a useful purpose in providing for the widely differing spiritual appetites of mankind. The greater the harmony produced within a society by the followers of a particular faith, the closer to God do those followers appear to the rest of the world.

Of the two wonderful Mormon friends I made while in Utah one was the scout executive of Ogden, Dilworth Young (grand nephew of Brigham) who, years later, became one of the chief leaders of the Mormon Church, a member of their Council of the Seventies. Once, after the war, at a dinner party in Dill's Salt Lake City home, one of the guests asked:

"Brother Dilworth, how come you haven't brought Starr into the church?"

Now Dill and I had often discussed religion and the Mormons' strong belief in conversion. He knew that I believed no church could claim to be the "only true church," which so many, including the Mormons, do indeed believe. But we both respected each others' viewpoint. Now, Dill looked at me, smiled and replied to his guest:

"Yes, people have asked me that often, before. Well, Starr and I have been friends for a long time. I have observed that he seems to have pretty good communication with God in his own way. Maybe he's just as good outside, on the steps of our church, as he would be inside of it. I wouldn't dream of imposing my will over his."

Yes, Dill was a great man. Discernment, such as his, was of the stuff of which genuine statesmen are made. How lucky I consider myself that those war years brought us together, and that I might call him friend.

My other close Mormon friend was an ebullient girl I met at the first dance given for our regiment the day after we arrived in Ogden. She was a member of that city's First Ward, and she invited me to go with her to one of their church's weekly "Firesides." These gatherings, held in different homes of the parish members, were attended by whole families—children, teenage youth and married couples of all ages. Led by a senior church member, acting as moderator, the evening was devoted to informal discussions of various aspects of the teachings of their religion, with emphasis on the particular way in which it related to their daily life. I found the procedure fascinating to listen to, especially when the younger ones would challenge their elders to be specific. They were little pragmatists, those kids, whose questing minds spurred their fathers and mothers, aunts and uncles, to search their hearts carefully. You knew from their replies that they were learning as much, or more, than their offspring. I understood, then, why Mormon families are so close-knit and why the practice of their religion was such a vital part of their everyday family life. It is perhaps their greatest contribution to the fiber of our society.

The second half of the Fireside evening was given over to refreshments and socializing, which I thoroughly enjoyed. It was a form of "dating" I had never experienced before—siting on a couch in a crowded room, chit-chatting about religion and the war, while with our eyes we explored each other's hearts. The "Firesides" were a weekly event and I became a regular visitor. We also had other dates—an occasional movie, with slow walks homeward from the theatre through snow-covered back streets that perhaps took us over-long to travel.

And, of course, on Sundays I would attend church with the young lady. We would sit together on the back row where we could converse in low tones without attracting attention, or so we hoped. But some friendly church member would accost us, after the service, offering to elaborate on some facet of the talks from the rostrum, which they had presumed we were discussing. Not wishing to disappoint these gentle people I would respond with sincere questions. I truly believe that from the ensuing conversations we all drew spiritual nourishment. Consequently, in the short ten weeks of my stay in Ogden, I received a liberal indoctrination in Mormon philosophy.

One element of Mormon thinking, which intrigued me, was their belief about God's purpose for man on this earth. To them, man has pre-existed this life. In that other world each soul waits entry to this world that he may acquire a human body which he will need in the next life to follow. And that "after life," they contend, will be a continuation of the experiences of this life, only on a higher plane of achievement. This philosophy accounts, in part, for their large families.

Such an interpretation of God's purpose (while still not satisfying my own seeking) seemed to carry more logical persuasion than the traditional Christian view that man is born a sinful creature, estranged from his Creator because of a vague sin committed by his first ancestor. Expressed simply, most Christians are taught that man's only purpose on earth is to find his way back into God's graces. That view has always bothered me because it defies reason. I feel certain that the

Creator of the universe simply must intend some greater goal for mankind.

While I touched on these matters with my newfound Mormon friends, I am not sure I made my viewpoint clear to them, particularly the young lady whom I was dating. But she did know that I was seeking, and I think she hoped I would find my answers in her own faith.

When, in March, I was ordered to report to Fort Benning, Georgia, for officer training she gave me a copy of the *Book of Mormon* which she said the members of her church wished me to have. I would find in it, they suggested, answers to much that was troubling me. I told her to thank them and say that I was genuinely sorry to leave, for they had been kind and gracious. Indeed, I respected them for the sincerity of their faith, and I had learned to love them for the warmth of their friendship.

On the train, as it pulled out from the Ogden station, I opened their book. It was inscribed "to Lieut. Starr Jones." Bless them, they had pre-supposed that I would successfully complete the three months' officer training, and so they beat the army's official salutation by many weeks. I let the book fall open on my lap, idly flipping the pages. Then, on the inside of the back cover, I noticed another inscription. In a graceful feminine hand my friend had written (in part): "For the church mouse in the back pew, there will always be..." I smiled to myself, remembering the admonition of her church friends that I would find answers in the book—was this also an answer? Was my lovely lady of the long walks down snow-covered back streets telling me something?

A few days later, at Fort Benning, I put her picture on my barracks room wall, along with the rest of my feminine rogue's gallery and placed the *Book of Mormon* in my foot locker. The next day I was plunged into a whirlwind of training and thought little about the matter for many months.

However, two years later when I received sudden orders for a special mission to the West Coast, I remembered. The movement was secret and I could not tell anyone where I was going. On the spot I made a decision that was to create a crisis in my own life. With trepidation I picked up my orders and reported for the assignment.

But, before that day arrived, through intensive months at Fort Benning, and later at Camp Gruber, I was to acquire many new skills, which drew on talents I never knew I possessed. In the process I learned that the essence of leadership, military or otherwise, lay not in an ability to issue orders, but in a capacity to anticipate crisis, to make on-the-spot decisions that resolved emergencies, and to develop in other people, confidence in their own self-reliance. Through all of this my feeling grew steadily that I was working at something vitally important in this stage of human progress. And my on-going dialogue with the Creator added measurably to this satisfaction. Paramount was a conviction that crisis is indeed a critical element in God's purpose for our lives. Certainly it played an important part in sharpening perceptions, and obviously there was nothing like the crisis of war to heighten one's awareness of values.

When I received my commission, in June of '42, I was already 36 years old and, by Army standards, considered too old for duty as a front-line infantry platoon leader, the job of a second lieutenant. So, I was assigned to Fort Benning's Infantry School as an instructor. In the next 18 months over 35,000 second lieutenants were graduated from our classes. During that time I rose to first lieutenant and then captain—a rank that would permit me to be assigned to combat troops.

Well, you can't watch a war to preserve human dignity and freedom spread across the world, train men to fight in it, and not get impatient to join them in the task—I was no exception. Twice I volunteered for hazardous duty: once to join Merrill's Marauders, and once a famous infantry outfit. But each time I was rejected—for the Marauders because the War Department in Washington thought that at 37 a man would be too old for that strenuous behind-the-lines Burma Mission; for the other outfit, simply because the Infantry School refused to release me from its staff of instructors. I suppose the Washington brass did not know that I was in excellent physical condition. I ran two miles each morning and made myself take frequent forced marches, on one of which I did 75 miles in 30 hours with full pack and rifle. On the other score the school valued me as an instructor because I was at home in the darkness and I taught courses on many night problems. So I had to keep on training men, men by the thousands who went to join combat units, most of whom I would never see again. However, one man, whose story I'll tell later because it makes a strong spiritual point, I did run into quite by accident, many years after the war.

Against this background my personal confrontations with God continued. He had created this world. I was involved in trying to preserve it, at least that part of it which was in my path. And for the moment that part was training men to preserve their own lives while taking others. History has shown that in times of war (or pestilence) more lives are ended abruptly than are created through normal birth patterns. The significance of these factors did not enter my consciousness during average work hours, because pressure was too intense, and there was scant time for reflection. But I did think about them, often as I was double-timing my two miles in semi-darkness before reveille each morning, and sometimes in the twilight hours when I would be waiting in the field for troops to assemble for night operations.

I remember one particular July evening out in the pine forest. I was waiting for dark to fall before beginning a class in identification of night noises—like the sounds of a match striking, a truck tailgate closing or bells tinkling to warn when barbed wire is being disturbed. Tonight, those bells started talking and I knew the sergeant responsible for that evening's work detail was checking the cowbells attached to the barbed wire under which the men must crawl. But to me, waiting in a meadow at the edge of the woods, the sound spoke of days at home on the farm. The mellow note of the cowbells evoked the warm scent of cattle standing at the pasture gate, waiting to be brought into the barn for milking. Milk, the universal food of life—how often I had squatted beside a heifer, my head against her flank, my hands deftly squeezing to bring the life-giving liquid squirting musically into the pail between my knees.

Tonight my thoughts turned to the young men who were even then moving up through the twilight to attend this training session. I would be teaching them how to stay alive, but also how to kill. How, I wondered, did such killing fit in to the Divine plan for purpose in this world? Scriptures enjoined us not to kill our brothers. Yet Scriptures were also filled with stories about our enemies who had to be annihilated in order that we should live; enemies who were poised to kill us unless we, in turn, destroyed them. And some Bible stories said that God would interfere, on our behalf, to slay our enemies. The obvious paradox of such conflicting philosophies troubled me.

Who really were our enemies? Were they the soldiers of the armies of the Axis nations now opposing us? Nations whose religious faith professed to believe in the same moral principles to which we subscribed? Or was the enemy actually a contrary, rebounding force, created by our own failure to practice the principles of behavior which our Judeo-Christian faith professed? It seemed to me that the Bible wasn't too clear on the matter of who were our enemies.

Finally, if the Bible was the absolute word of God how was it possible that it contained contradictory guidelines? Or was the Bible merely a collection of the writings of man, inspired by God? Both views are held by different churches, today. So, which is right? I had often heard the subject discussed but never, satisfactorily, resolved. Now, waiting in the gathering darkness on the edge of a Georgia pine forest, I started to call on my Creator to enlighten me—and then I did not. For no sooner had the thought crossed my mind than I knew God would make me answer it, myself, with His gentle probing:

"What seems logical, my son?"

I smiled to myself. In the 20-plus years of our sporadic dialogue I had come to expect this nudge to use the native intelligence (some call it common sense) with which God has endowed me, though sometimes I've had to dig deep to uncover it from the debris of careless thoughts that frequently tend to smother it.

Well, it didn't take lengthy analysis to convince myself that if contradictions existed anywhere in the Bible such fact threw doubt on the validity of the whole as being the irrefutable word of God. Which, in the last analysis, made sense, too, because very few words mean exactly the same in every language. That factor alone is a constant problem to translators, and the Bible has undergone many, many translations. Very well then, I would regard the Bible as only recording man's reaching out to touch the source of Creation: a history written by sincere men, many of them undoubtedly inspired by God—though why the record ceased to be made for the last two thousand years leaves an uncomfortable hiatus. Therefore, when the Judaic-Christian Scriptures fail to provide spiritual guidelines which seem to me logical or adequate for modern times, I am forced to look elsewhere among the many other sacred writings of man.* And, failing that, I will search deep in my own heart, as I have so many times in the past.

Thus the question, "Who are my enemies?" remained for the time being an unresolved spiritual enigma. For, now, I would have to content myself with the traditional military designation of *"an opposing hostile force or person."* And, though I had reached no satisfactory resolution within my own mind, as to how God's purpose for this world was served by men killing each other in wars, I knew I would keep pursuing the question with the Creator. Perhaps, if I finally got into battle myself, He would show me answers. Until then I would follow the pragmatic dictum which holds that it's not how you die, but how you live, that really counts.

Yet, even as I was preparing men to take lives, I was becoming increasingly aware of the need for creation of new life. Up until now, while I had been searching for spiritual purpose in life, I had been overlooking the most obvious of man's intended physical purposes, propagation of the species. So far, as a carefree bachelor, I had not felt impelled to do anything about it. In fact, the pressures of social custom discouraged bringing new life into being outside of wedlock. This view I had no quarrel with, for the idea of irresponsible parenting had been as repugnant to me then as it still is today. But the war years had brought the possibility of exit from this planet into daily focus, thus increasing my concern about leaving without passing on to future generations the genes that had come down to me from my ancestors, as well as those of my own individuality.

*The Koran, The Vedas, The Analects of Confucius.

Though I saw wartime marriages taking place all about me I had not been moved to consider taking that plunge myself. During the seven years of off-again on-again romance with the beautiful young actress for whom I had first propelled myself across the country, I had dated many other lovely ladies. Yet none of them had I courted seriously. Perhaps this was because I still held to a sentimental dream about first love. But that fantasy had finally terminated one night in November of '43 when she telephoned to say she was getting married the next day. For a wild instant I contemplated tearing up to New York to remonstrate, but military leave was impossible at that moment and I had no taste to go "over-the-hill." Lives were dependent on my being where I was. Thus ended, abruptly, one period of my emotional life.

Five weeks later, at the request of a general of the 42d Infantry Rainbow Division, I was finally released from my duties at Fort Benning and assigned to the 42d at Camp Gruber, Oklahoma. I reported there in January of 1944, and on Thanksgiving of that year, we sailed for combat duty in France. At last, I thought, I will be heading into the eye of the storm which has engulfed the world. Surely, somewhere in that awful fury, God will have further answers for me on the questions of violent death.

But that January, when I reported for duty with the Rainbow, I was overdue a full month's leave. However, due to increased demands from the battlefields of Europe, it was not forthcoming, and I was plunged into the most intense work schedule I had yet experienced. General Harry J. Collins, our Division Commander, had a reputation for being a master at training combat troops. I soon learned why. We were up before reveille and out in the field all day on combat problems, obstacle courses, forced marches, range firing. Meals were often served in the field. When the weary enlisted men hit the sack at taps, the officers continued till midnight with exercises in map reading, troop movements and logistics, many of which I helped to create, and then taught. No time for recreation or dating now, but certainly few divisions entered combat better prepared than ours.

Then, one afternoon in the middle of April, our regimental executive officer sent for me.

"Jones," he said, "We're sending a detachment of soldiers to the West Coast. Their destination is secret; they're wearing no insignia. I need a captain to act as escort officer. You were overdue for leave when you came here. We can't give you leave, even now, but the escort officer on this mission will be allowed eleven days delay in reporting back here after delivering the troops train at the port of embarkation. Will you take the assignment?"

"Will I take it? Eleven days to do what I want! Sir, when do I leave?"

The Major grinned and slapped me on the back. "You go tonight. It's a three-car train. You'll have two sergeants to help you. You must not tell anyone. No phone calls until after you deliver the troops. Understand?"

"Yes, sir."

"Good, I'm glad we can give you this break. Use the time well."

I returned to my barracks, put what items I'd need into a small Val Pac, then stood for a moment and looked at the lovely faces on my rogue's gallery wall.

Which girls would I have time to look up? Dining, dancing—the prospect set my blood tingling. Suddenly a wild idea hit me. I closed my eyes, said a short prayer, then opened them and looked again at the photographs on the wall.

The exciting redhead in Hollywood, at whose garage my library was stored? The almost too young (17 years my junior) but mentally tantalizing brunette in Utah? She lived somewhat out of my way, but I could route my return trip through Salt Lake. Or the candy blonde in Beverly Hills? Maybe even some of the other pretty ladies whose charms had kept me writing letters. I deliberated for a moment, re-opened my foot locker and added one last item to my Val Pac. Then I reported to the railhead and was soon rolling westward.

The train did not reach the coast until the second day following. Outside of stops at certain towns for meals, where we would march the men, in formation, to and from a pre-arranged restaurant location, there was little for my sergeants and myself to do other than check the cars periodically. But the soldiers, after months of exhaustive training, seemed glad of the opportunity to just rest, relax and enjoy the scenery flashing by. I'm sure many of them were thinking seriously about what lay ahead for them in the far-flung reaches of the Pacific battlefields. As indeed I was also, though I had no way of knowing yet exactly where I, myself, would engage the enemy.

Ah, there was that word again—the enemy. Through the train window I looked beyond the pastoral countryside toward the distant horizon. Focusing my eyes at

the point where land met sky I once more reached out
with my mind to communicate with my Creator:

"No, Lord," I said, "I'm not asking you, again, to define
the enemy for me. I know that question will be resolved in due
time. Today, all I'm asking is that you help these fine young
men, riding with me, to acquit themselves bravely, and with
compassion, when they meet those who have proclaimed
themselves our adversaries. Now, that may not be a proper
prayer for those who have got to kill or be killed, but please
accept it anyway."

The spot on the horizon now seemed to blur so that I
could not tell exactly where sky fell or earth rose up to
meet the heavenly vault, and the click of the rails punc-
tuated my thoughts like twin shots from a rifle that
seemed never to run out of ammunition.

"And while I'm on the subject of prayer, Lord, you know I
don't believe in asking favors for myself, yet I do need guidance. Please be over my shoulder when I call upon those
young ladies—they are so lovely—don't let my need override
their own intended destinies."

Next day, the soldiers were detrained at Fort Ord. I
formed them up along the railroad siding and looked
them over, full in the eyes of each man, as I moved
down the line. Such a fine group. Many of their faces I
had seen, dirty and sweaty, struggling through some of
the training exercises I had conducted.

God, I hoped they would remember those vital drill-
ings when the chaos of battle swirled over them. "Good
luck," I said. Then I turned the detail over to the reception officer and watched as the sergeants marched the
detachment off toward the main post. Behind me

the empty train backed away from the siding and I was alone.

My next move should be to headquarters to secure my clearances, after which I would be free to make phone calls. But I lingered there, beside the rails, a wave of nostalgia taking hold of me as I watched the gulls, in the sky beyond the tracks, wheeling gracefully over Monterey Bay. How long had it been since I'd first come to this same encampment as a raw recruit? "Just a bunch of dumb civilians," so the regular Army sergeant had contemptuously referred to our group of early draftees. Three full years ago it was, this very month of April—it seemed an eternity, and now I'd come full circle.

I looked again at the low hills between myself, the beach, and the waters of the Pacific. On one of those same hillocks I'd stood at sunset one evening soon after I'd arrived. With hungry heart I'd reached out to bring the Creator's countenance into my view, only to turn and find Him smiling at me through the eyes of a young boy. That moment of insight had heightened every hour of the three years since then. It had enabled me to reach cooperation with many a man with whom I had otherwise no communication, and we both, as well as the country we served, benefited by the contact. I had found it fascinating, this watching for glimpses of the Divine countenance in the eyes of people. Sometimes we might be casually chatting together, or relaxing over coffee and a drink, or even while dancing—especially dancing. For then conversation is unnecessary, then just eye contact can translate music and movement into pure poetry, and poetry is a cord that can pull aside curtains.

Dancing—the thought broke the spell of my reverie. Roused now, I hastened to the adjutant's office to complete the paperwork involved in clearance. By late afternoon I was free and on the telephone. I called the redhead first because my Ford Coupe was stored in her garage along with my books. Los Angeles is a city of magnificent distances and it is difficult to get about without an automobile.

"It's wonderful to hear from you," her surprised voice answered. "Where are you?"

"Just north of L.A.," I replied. "Can you have dinner with me in about two and a half hours?"

"Oh, yes! But..."

"But what?"

"I've just come from the beauty parlor and my hair is all in curlers!"

"Well stuff it under one of those pretty hats of yours."

"My train gets into L.A. Station at 8:00. Can you meet me there?"

I stood outside on the platform of the train for most of the trip down. April in California is spring and the fragrance from fields and orchards delighted my senses as the iron wheels hurtled us through the twilight. Especially tantalizing was the smell of orange blossoms— that intoxicating perfume so like the fragrances of stately lilies or the lowly, trailing arbutus.

She was waiting at the station, wearing a stunning turquoise coat-suit, but no hat covered her beautifully curled red hair.

I took her hand and turned her around admiringly. "But you told me curlers?" I said.

"I rushed back to Irene's. Between dryer and hand brushing we managed. Did you actually think I'd come down that way?"

We had supper at a little Mexican place in Olivera Street. For the next several days she took French leave from her job at Pacific Airmotive, and we drove, and ate, and talked. She had asked once, when I was first commissioned, to come visit me at Fort Benning, but I hadn't let her. Now I tried to fill her in on all that had transpired during those two years. Before I knew it, my leave time was half gone and I had not yet contacted any of my other girlfriends.

The next day she returned to her work at the aircraft offices and I spent the day bringing myself to face the crisis I knew was developing. For several hours I drove about the city. A good part of the time I was praying deeply, sincerely praying, as I had not prayed since my father died and I had felt so sad for his shortened life. Now I prayed for insight, that I might do what was best for this girl whose eyes looked at me so disconcertingly. In a few weeks, a matter of months at most, I would be overseas and fighting. I had already seen many young girls widowed before they had hardly had a chance to become acquainted with their young husbands. Some had babies, too, who would never know the touch of their father's hand. That fact was doubly sad to me because I'd come to the point in my life where I really wanted to have children of my own. But not, I felt, under those circumstances. Such a union seemed totally unfair to either the pre-orphaned child or to its young mother.

I kept on driving, and praying, and several times almost stopped at a church to continue the effort. But that day the California sun, casting its warmth over the moving multitudes on the sidewalks and streets of the city, seemed, somehow, to pull me closer to God than the cool, empty inside of a church building. So I continued driving.

My prayers were clumsy, for it was not until many years later that I learned the real secret of prayers, and today they lacked the flow which had marked my other conversations with the Creator. For me it was always harder to ask for something straight out, like I was trying to do now. But finally God had compassion on my struggling mind and He began answering me:

> *"What did you tell yourself when you looked at those pictures on your barrack's wall?"*
> "You know, Lord," I said. "I'm wasting my life. The fact, that I don't have a wife to share it with, to inspire me, to raise a family with."
> *"Then why do you hesitate now?"*
> "Because I don't want my life to become a burden to anyone."
> *"And why should it be? Isn't it her privilege to make a decision about that?"*
> The Lord's voice was soft as the afternoon breeze.
> *"Have you forgotten, my son, your own discovery that the human heart requires challenge to grow on? You owe her the chance. Besides, she may not want you after all."*

Well, I'd certainly asked for that one. It broke the somber note of my preoccupation and I chuckled to myself as I stopped the car, checked street signs and map to find out just where I'd got to in my rambling drive.

In another hour I had picked her up at her place of work and we went out to supper together. Later that evening I proposed to her. Looking deep into those challenging brown eyes I was sure I saw the Divine shutter blink, and I closed my own eyes in a quick prayer of thanks. Then I took out the small jewel box which I'd taken from my footlocker before leaving and offered the diamond ring to Virginia.

Two days later we headed for Yuma, Arizona, by way of a dear friend's ranch in Escondido at the base of Mt. Palomar. The next morning Ginny picked her wedding bouquet of enormous California roses in Carrol's garden, and we drove off in the early dawn. Driving through a lonely stretch of mountains we stopped to pray at a small Spanish mission.

We arrived in Yuma at 11:00 a.m. and went straight to the court house. As luck would have it, Ginny stumbled as we climbed the many steps. Remembering, I am sure, the old cliche that stumbling upstairs means you won't get married that year, Ginny looked at me almost in tears. "Don't worry," I said, "that doesn't apply here. We'll get married."

But we almost didn't make it. As we were leaving the clerk's window after purchasing our marriage license, I noticed a tall, thin man in a black suit standing by the door. As we passed him he reached out and offered me his calling card. He represented a "marriage parlor," one of those commercial enterprises which, for a graduating fee, will provide a justice of the peace, witnesses, flowers, organ music and other material appurtenances of a traditional wedding ceremony. There were a number of such "quickie" establishments in

Yuma. But the thought of their cold commercialism made us shudder, as did the tall, thin man in his black suit. We thanked him and went in search of a church.

Locating St. Paul's Episcopal Church, the housekeeper at the rectory informed us that the pastor, the Rev. Bancroft Smith, was out on a parish call but due back real soon. Graciously she invited us to come in. For the next two and a half hours we waited in the rectory parlor, alternately holding hands or chatting with the gentle housekeeper, a romantically inclined soul, who bustled in and out every little while assuring us: "He'll be here soon. Don't you go away!"

But as the time dragged on, Ginny, remembering that stumble up those court house steps, became more and more uneasy. Were the fates against us? Would we have to go back to that unattractive thin man and his marriage parlor? We couldn't wait till the next day. There were just enough hours now to drive back to Oklahoma to report for duty on time. Inside myself I was telling God that since I'd followed His leading, I hoped He would not let me down now. Then I just squeezed Ginny's hand tighter and tried to look reassuring.

Finally, the young clergyman returned. But when we explained our wishes he was reluctant to marry us that day. He would need a letter from the pastor of our own church, he said. If we would just wait a few days... I could see he was temporizing, he felt it his duty to discourage hasty marriages, particularly since Yuma was one of the few places in the United States which required no waiting time between issuance of a marriage license and performance of the ceremony. He was apologetic but firm.

"I'm sorry," I told the good minister. "I respect your position, but if you can't do it then we'll just have to use one of those grim marriage parlors in town. It's too bad. We did want a church wedding. My own father was an Episcopal clergyman. But if it can't be, we'll hope God understands and will be with us anyway."

The Rev. Mr. Smith smiled in defeat. "Do you have witnesses with you?" When I nodded negatively the hovering housekeeper quickly volunteered that, "Sergeant Watson and his wife are right next door. I'll get them at once." Then she hurried away and the Rev. Mr. Smith proceeded to fill out the necessary papers.

So, with the late Arizona sun streaming in the open doors of the little brown-shingled church, Ginny, accompanied by the sergeant's wife (also a Virginia) walked smilingly up the aisle to where I, with Sgt. Watson and the Rev. Mr. Smith on either side of me, waited at the altar rail. And we knew that God, too, was smiling on our marriage. Our one regret was that we had no music, for the organist was out of town that afternoon. But the music of the spheres has played gently in the background of our lives ever since.

That night we slept at the Adam Hotel in Phoenix, and two days later we drove into Camp Gruber. I went to the Regimental Headquarters to turn in an official request for "Married Officer's Quarters." The adjutant, Capt. Mould, looked up from the paper in surprise:

"You didn't?" he exclaimed.
"I certainly did," I replied.

Later that day I reported to Maj. Fitzpatrick who had given me the escort mission. I told him that I had followed his advice and made the best possible use of the eleven-day delay allowed to me. Indeed, the years which followed have proved it beyond my fondest hopes. It has been a truly wonderful marriage. Though we were not blessed with children until over four years later, it was actually 10 months after coming off of active duty before our babies began arriving. Then: one, two, three, four—almost in cadence—in four and a half years, our four sons were born.

However, we could not see that far ahead then and we treasured our few short hours together each week. Under ordinary times we would have had Saturday afternoons and Sundays off, to spend at our rented house in the town of Muskogee, just 10 miles from Gruber. But now the stepped-up training program kept us "on post" almost 24 hours a day. Our wives were nicknamed "Muskogee Widows." The regimental commander tried to ease our situation by inviting the wives to eat with us at the Officer's Mess on Wednesday and Saturday nights. We were lucky to get home for a few hours sleep one night a week.

In late August, along with five other captains from the Division, I was detailed to take a field commanders' course at the Army's Command and General Staff School in Fort Leavenworth, Kansas. This was a most fortuitous break for Ginny and myself because Leavenworth was just across the river from Sugar Lake, Missouri, where Ginny's parents had a summer cottage—and I did have Sundays off from classes. Those were indeed rewarding days. I got to know Ginny's wonderful dad and mother, her sister Kate and Kate's dynamic husband Pete. We fished, boated, swam and enjoyed each other's company. Ginny's dad, who was a locomotive engineer with the Burlington Railroad, taught me how to fire the big coal-burning engines and to drive them. I was an eager pupil thinking, who knows in some combat situation the skill might prove useful! Those three exciting months passed all too quickly.

Suddenly, in mid-November, a telegram recalled us to Gruber. The Division had been ordered overseas. Within a few more days our three infantry regiments moved out. Wives and families departed for their respective homes. Ginny returned to Los Angeles to work and wait, and it would be two and a half years before I saw her again. Our troop trains rolled east to Camp Kilmer, New Jersey, the staging area for units destined to serve in the European Theatre of Operations.

The day the regiment boarded ship, our battalion was marched in company formation to a huge wharfside warehouse. The last shakedown had been completed. The men carried full battle equipment, but all unit identifications had been removed—division patches, regimental numbers, even officer and noncom insignias—all these had been taken off because such markers help the enemy pick off leaders, and to know exactly which units they are opposing. In my hand was a roster listing the 285 men of Company K, which I was commanding. Even from those lists we had carefully cut out all identifying numbers, just in case the lists should fall into enemy hands. But we knew who we were, who our commanders were, and we still had our name tags on the right pocket of our battle fatigues.

As I looked over the hundreds of men, quietly waiting to board ship, I found myself praying:

"Lord, this is it, now. Help us to keep our courage, a sense of honor and, if it be possible in this day and age, a sense of chivalry."

My prayer thoughts were interrupted at that moment by loudspeakers on the wall which began barking out orders:

"All units attention! Everyone, enlisted and officers, put down your equipment where you are, strip naked, everything off! When that is done, face right and move in column file to the right. As you pass the medical inspecting team raise your arms above your heads. Keep moving. Commanders, make sure *every man* goes with the column. Ready now, commence disrobing!"

In minutes the area had come noisily alive as hundreds of puzzled men dropped equipment and peeled off their clothes. Soon columns of naked men, their arms uplifted to the rafters, were dancing past the waiting medical teams. Never in my life had I witnessed such an incongruous scene. Gone was every vestige of individual identification. The battalion commander looked no different than any of the privates. The 1200-plus men of the battalion were like a giant herd of grinning apes, their arms upraised in some wild, tribal dance.

I could not keep from laughing as, in my own turn, I passed the battalion surgeon who was eyeing each man's armpits and genitals.

"What are you looking for, Doc?"
"Body lice, soldier."

"Are we supposed to have cooties?" Lieutenant Carl Miller, my company executive officer, asked of no one in particular.

"We hope not, soldier," called out one of the medical team. "'Cause if you do, the whole ship will be scratching like hell before we land. Those little bastards multiply fast."

The whole process was over in thirty minutes, and the men, having replaced their garments and recovered their identities, now swung packs and rifles to shoulders and moved out onto the wharf to begin boarding.

Later that night I stood on the foredeck of the now loaded troop-ship and watched a flickering glow on the underside of the overcast sky, caused by the neon lights of New York City's theatre district only a few miles to the north of us. Somewhere, under that haze of vibrating illumination I knew my own sister waited word from me, little suspecting I was so close by, and even at that moment moving off toward a rendezvous with the unknown. I had hoped for a chance to get into New York to see her, but it was not to be. Well, I thought to myself, she doesn't know I'm here, or where I'm going. But the enemy did know, though I did not find out the unusual source of their information until many weeks after hostilities were ended.

Before going below to rejoin my company, quartered on deck G deep in the hold, I thought to conclude my

conversation with the Creator which I'd broken off
when the loudspeakers interrupted:

> "Excuse the interruption, Lord. I was really very serious
> about what I was saying before that public address system
> sounded off, but it was so funny. I don't think I'll ever forget
> those hundreds of naked men performing that cootie dance.
> Oh, Lord, we must surely present you with some hilarious situ-
> ation at times."
> *"You do indeed, my son."*
> "Should we apologize?"
> *"Not unless you think laughter is unimportant."*
> "Oh no, Lord. Without laughter how could we live with
> some of the mistakes we make? Or, to presume the logic you
> press me with, how else could You, Lord, refrain sometimes,
> from anger with us?"
> *"So you are learning, my son."*
> "I know, Lord, that laughter heals the spirit. Also, that it is
> the leaven of wisdom, and a last bulwark against despair."
> *"You could do well to carry such conclusions with you in the*
> *days ahead, my son."*
> "Yes, Lord. I'll try not to forget."

I left the deck then, and climbed down the long iron
ladder toward the lower hold. And as I went, I was
sure the Lord was calling after me that I should not
forget, either, to turn that laughter, frequently, upon
myself.

With the possibility of being torpedoed at any moment, boat drill was a regular and serious business.
Each day, at the signal for boat drill, the men of our
Company K (two-thirds of them seasick) would duti-
fully mount the stairway leading to the lifeboats, six
decks above. But movement up was always slow,
when halfway up it would cease altogether. Finally,
without ever having reached the pure, clear air of the

boat deck, the drill would end and the men would return, wearily, to their bunks.

One day, General Linden, our task force commander, came jogging down the ladder on a spot inspection. The men stood rigidly at attention while the general glanced casually at their bunks, equipment and uniforms. Suddenly, without preliminary, he turned to one of the men and spat out a question:

"Soldier, which way is north?"

The bewildered, seasick GI, who hadn't been above deck since we sailed, looked first at the general, then at his buddies and then at me. I gave him a wink and he turned back to the general, quickly pointing his finger to the general's rear, he snapped out.

"That way, Sir!"
"That's what I like to hear!"   The general smiled broadly.
"This man doesn't know where north is anymore than I do, but he's got a positive answer.   He'll make out in combat!"

With that the general spun around and bounded up the ship's stairway out of our sight, while the men relaxed into hearty laughter.

Thirteen days later our convoy of ships reached Marseille Harbor on the south of France. Here the grim reality of war hit us hard—a mass of half–submerged, wrecked ships. The unhappy remains of the French Navy completely clogged the harbor. Nothing could move in or out. Our American ships were forced to disembark thousands of soldiers onto an outjutting breakwater and we marched, two-by-two, over that narrow, mile-long causeway to dry land. From thence by train (till the tracks were blown up) and then by truck, we moved up to the battle front, reaching Strasbourg, France, on the twenty third of December.

The next day, Christmas Eve of 1944, at 4:00 p.m., I led my Company K to positions along the Rhine River on the left flank of Strasbourg, where we relieved another American unit already dug-in on the extensive grounds of a large French estate. The soldiers we were relieving withdrew before dark and we settled into the bunkers and foxholes with rifles ready. By 7:00 p.m., we recorded our first casualty, and the Germans were calling to us, from across the Rhine River, "Hello Rainbow!" How they learned our identity, after all our laborious efforts at secrecy, we did not know, but we answered them with rifle fire. It was a grim Christmas Eve which none of us would ever forget.

I mention these details here because they are the background for one of those oft-repeated battle stories which are actually myths.

I first heard the story after World War I, when it was reported that on Christmas Eve the soldiers of both sides left their positions and, meeting in no-man's land between the trenches, sang Christmas carols together. Such a romantic story is bound to re-surface many times and probably did, too, even before World War I, and so it did after World War II, in the late 1950's. I was an editor then with a magazine in New York. We received a manuscript from a man who claimed he was an Army chaplain and he wanted to tell us a true story that happened to him in World War II.

Then he proceeded to repeat the Christmas Eve story about Germans and Americans leaving their weapons and their positions to sing carols between the lines. This he said he observed as he moved through the lines on the night of December 24, 1944, and he described the place where it occurred—along the Rhine River on the northern outskirts of Strasbourg—the exact location where I and the men of my Company K were stationed. Of course it had not happened. It could not have happened. The soldiers of Company K would have shot anyone trying to move anywhere through our lines. And we were occupying an extended frontage, a distance normally assigned to a battalion. That's a lot of territory. No, the writer of the Christmas Eve legend could not have observed Americans and Germans caroling together there, because it did not occur. The story was a myth.

I returned the manuscript to the author, explaining the impossibility of the occurrence. We never heard from him again. My guess is that it was sent by some enterprising writer (chaplain or not) who thought to cash in on the oft-repeated legend by claiming he was there. How could he have known when he mailed it out that the editor who would receive the manuscript would have been the officer commanding the very unit stationed at the spot where he claimed the event took place.

I relate this incident, not to discredit some unknown writer's attempt to give new life to a lovely religious legend, but to illustrate how easily writers, with the best of intentions, can misrepresent or distort the facts. Particularly when many years elapse, and especially when the subject concerns emotional or religious values. This has been the reason for my own reluctance to accept everything in the Bible as being the literal word of God. Such acquiescence is contrary to my understanding of the rule of logic.

Of course, I realize, even as I write this, that the same charge may be leveled at my own efforts. In defense of which I can only say that I have been scrupulously careful in reporting events as they actually occurred in my life. The thoughts which streamed through my consciousness at the time, I have tried to recapture, now, and put into words, many for the first time.

And so, that Christmas of 1944, I was thrust into the reality of battle, into the eye of that chaotic maelstrom about which, up until then, I had had to rely on the written and verbal reports of other people, people who had actually experienced combat. I hoped the skills which three and a half years of training had built into my body and mind would prove equal to the challenges, and I prayed to God I would be able to exercise wise leadership. Beyond that, I prayed sincerely for further spiritual insights.

I was not reluctant to do battle. I was convinced of the need to oppose the human forces who had plunged our world into global conflict. But I longed to know more about how such conflict fitted into divine purpose, for I was unwilling to blame the waste of war on any vague "Force of Evil." As far as I was concerned, such thinking was a cop-out for human responsibility. More than ever before I looked upon this earth, and everything in it, as God's creation, with logical purpose behind the totality of human experience. For me the challenge now lay in unlocking the secret of the relationships.

The major Allied effort of the winter campaign had required all available troops to contain the fury of the Bulge, the last German counteroffensive of the war. The demand of that struggle scraped the bottom of the barrel for every available combat unit still in the United States. Such green troops, our Rainbow Division was one of them, were rushed overseas to hold the frontline positions vacated by troops taken out to contain the enemy at the Bulge. In our sector, battle-hardened veterans of the Italian and African campaign had been moved to the southern flank of the Bulge at Metz, some 30 miles northeast of Strasbourg. We assumed their area of responsibility.

Our own baptism of fire came quickly as General Von Rundstet's corps crossed the Rhine River to engage our extended front. From the fifth to the twentieth of January 1945, our Rainbow would attack, withdraw, move to new positions and attack again. In those furious weeks I gained new insight into the bond which draws individuals into the solidarity of family unity.

In peacetime living, the average civilian may get to know intimately, perhaps not more than 20 or 30 persons in a lifetime. Outside of his immediate family, the group he cares about, and who care about him, will consist of a few close friends and, over the years, maybe a dozen fellow workers—they are the individuals with whom he shares dreams, joys and grief. They are his extended family, held together by an invisible force. However, in this case, the glue is not, in the terms of playwright O'Neill, the grace of God but, rather, the adhesive of shared goals, shared purpose in life.

By contrast the military man, especially in wartime, is more fortunate than the average civilian because his circle of close friends is greater. Because the soldier must live in daily close contact with upwards of 200 individuals in his unit, eating together, working together for a common purpose, there are more people who care what happens to him—his extended family is more powerful. And people's horizons are broadened, their lives enriched, by close contact with other people's lives. It is one of the intangible rewards of military service. This important truth I had already become well acquainted with in my stateside years of non-combat service. Now, leading some of those same men through the rush and chaos of battle I would experience the supreme strength which grows out of sharing a common purpose.

In the battle of Gambsheim, on January 5, our Company K attacked down a spit of land between a canal and the Rhine, wiped out machine gun positions and captured nine Germans, the first prisoners to be taken by our Division. Our only casualty was a bullet in one soldier's ankle. Together, my company messenger and I formed a chair lift with our hands and wrists and carried him back to the lines at dusk. A few days later, attacking at dawn through a snowstorm, K Company helped re-establish the Allied position on the Moder River. Casualty: lost one advance scout, an American Indian lad from Oklahoma. But I had great confidence in the self-reliance of this man and felt sure he would turn up again. Sure enough he did—almost three months later. Having lost track of us in the snowstorm, he ended that day fighting with another regiment, with whose men he remained until our unit's paths crossed again during the push through Germany.

On January 18, from a position in the Sessenheim Woods on an outpost sector of the Maginot line, we were attacked by German units of twice our number. But Company K held, with the men fighting like veterans, though we sustained our worst casualties in this battle. Two days later, moving again, this time under artillery fire, we established our company in the village of Haganeau. With my platoon leaders we made reconnaissance to occupy advanced positions the next day. But, by dark, orders had come to fall back. The Division was straightening its line, and we had gone too far forward.

The battalion pulled out that night through the Haganeau Forest, light snow squalls contending with a hide-and-seek moon as our long column moved down a road between tall trees. Company K was assigned to protect the battalion's rear. I placed one of our machine gun crews in a jeep, to make sure we would not be surprised by any enemy following us, and put teams of riflemen well out among the trees on our flanks. Plodding along through the night, rifles cradled in our arms at the ready, some men I'm sure were half asleep as they walked. I was not surprised for we had been almost constantly on the move for over two weeks—

changing positions, attacking and moving on again. Once, one of the men had asked me:

"Captain, why do they keep moving us every few hours?"

"The top brass hasn't told me," I replied, "but I suspect they're trying to confuse the enemy."

"Well, they must be succeeding," said the rifleman," because even I'm as confused as hell!"

Later that night, checking again on the rear of the column I discovered the jeep was gone, but the machine gun crew were trudging along as though nothing had happened.

"Where's the jeep?" I asked the squad leader.

"Went off the road, got stuck on a big stone. We rocked and rocked but couldn't get it off."

"How far back?"

"Maybe three, four miles."

"We'll have to send someone back for it."

"They can't drive it, Captain. Oil pan's cracked."

"Damn!" I looked at the men closely. "Where are the machine guns?" The squad leader pointed rearward to where one man was pulling some sort of bundle over the snow. In the darkness I looked closer. Tied to an improvised sled of boughs were the two light machine guns.

"What kind of protection is that for the column? You'd be killed before you could get those guns into action! And where's the ammunition?"

"It was too heavy, we couldn't carry it."

"You left it on the jeep!" I was furious.

"We're beat out, Captain. We've had no sleep."

"You'll sleep in hell if the Jerries overtake us," I replied, then checked myself.

Anger would not correct our now exposed rear. These young soldiers, not over 20 years old any of them, had reached what they thought was their limit, and the squad leader had proved unequal to the moment. In four weeks of fighting over exhausting winter terrain this was the first link in our company's command to demonstrate weakness. I looked at the young sergeant:

> "Have you got any ammunition?"
> "No Sir, I—we..."

"Yes we have, Sir!" called out one of the men as he shuffled forward in the snowy road. When he came closer in the darkness I recognized the short, heavyset soldier. He had joined our Company the night before we shipped out, an older man, probably in his late thirties, a somewhat punch-battered ex-boxer. He had come to us with a group of less than physically fit draftees (one had clubbed feet, others had various handicaps that normally disqualified them for combat duty). They were men scraped together to fill up the ranks of the units being hurriedly shipped out to help contain the Bulge.

Now I saw that this man's normally chunky body was more than usually broad tonight, for over his shoulders were hung many belts of machine gun bullets, and in each hand he carried the regulation steel box filled with more belts of ammunition.

> "I went back and·got 'em, Captain, when I realized they'd been left."

"Good man." I said with relief. Then turning back to the reluctant squad leader I told him, "Come on, get that ammo redistributed to your men, and get those machine guns untied. You're damn lucky there's one soldier in your squad with guts enough to carry on even if he is dead tired. See that your guns are hand carried and trigger ready for the remainder of this march!"

Leaving the machine-gun squad leader to reorganize himself and his men I moved out through the forest to contact the weapons platoon leader whom I had assigned to supervise the flank guards. As I tramped through the soft snow, alert for possible enemy patrols, I was rehearsing to myself ways in which I could further train and inspire the men to greater effort in overcoming physical exhaustion. This machine gun incident was the first evidence of weakness. In more than four weeks on the front line the men of Company K had acquitted themselves with valor, fought fearlessly and responded to crisis with initiative and tenacity. When we went on the line Christmas Eve, we were a group of well-trained, but battle-ignorant individuals. Coming off the line now, we were a close-knit family of combat-toughened kinsmen. I was proud of them.

Following the Haganeau withdrawal, all three infantry regiments of our Rainbow Task-Force-Linden were brought together at La Wantzaneau for reorganization. Casualties among line officers (lieutenants and captains) had been heavy. Company K had lost three of our four lieutenants. In the reshuffle, now, I was moved up to command of our regimental headquarters company. Lt. Dave Zillmer (West Point 44) took over Command of Company K. I was sorry to leave them.

In late February we went on the line again, occupying defensive positions near Wimineau, France. On March 20, I was at regimental headquarters when word came from Division that was to make a dramatic change in the winter's campaign. As soon as the colonel had relayed the orders to his staff the battalion commanders left for their units. I, myself, headed for the half-finished log dugout in a forest hillside where my own company officers alerted by my messenger, were waiting. Squatting around me in the late spring sunshine, they waited, their faces reflecting tension and curiosity. "Take notes," I told them brusquely. "Tomorrow our 42d Division, together with units of all Allied armies across the entire Western front, will launch a coordinated attack to breach the Siegfried Line and carry the war into the German homeland."

The men looked up from their notes eagerly. This was it, the moment we had been waiting for! Just as Allied invasion troops had crossed the Channel in June of 1944, to meet the German might on the continent of Europe, so, now, the Allied armies, from the North Sea to the Swiss border would drive them back to final defeat. In the chaos and tragedy of war this was one of the few moments of elation. At 7:45 p.m. on March 21 the first elements of the Rainbow Division jumped off and the race for Berlin, Frankfurt and Munich was on.

The pace was furious. We crossed the Rhine River on pontoon bridges on Easter Sunday, took the city of Wurtzburg under heavy fire, then swung northeast to attack the German center of ball-bearing manufacture, the city of Schweinfurt. It was ringed with German 88s, a vicious artillery weapon that was often used for point blank fire, like a monster rifle with the impact of a bomb. Driving south, we took Furth while its twin city, Nuremburg, was burning. Once, when German resistance brought our advance to a halt, our division artillery were lined up hub-to-hub in a great field. All night long the guns fired without letup. In the morning we moved on, unhindered.

On another night a late halt in the Division's advance found my company looking for shelter from the rain in a bombed-out village. My jeep driver found a church with its front blown out, but sufficient roof remaining over the altar end to provide a dry area for rest.

"You don't mind sleeping in a church do you, Captain?" he asked.

"Of course not," I replied. "I've slept through sermons with no ill effects."

A few hours later the breaking dawn enabled us to see the reality of where we had rested. A few feet from where I had been lying a large statue of Christ on the Cross was tilted at a precarious angle above the altar. Once again I found myself wondering why the church insists on perpetuating the gentle Carpenter in attitudes of pain? It is such a negative viewpoint, belying the joy men should feel in sharing the creativity of God on this planet.

My driver brought up the jeep and waited patiently. Still I stood looking at what remained of the church, my eyes focused on that tilted cross, my mind absorbed in continuing debate with the Creator. For I was beginning to understand, why I had for so long been at odds with Christian theology, as promulgated in the

Gospel of St. John. I saw that Christianity had side-stepped man's responsibility for carrying forward God's continuing evolution of the physical world in which we live, and the cross, with its unhappy figure, had become the symbol of man's rejection of this world. The whole idea had lain, for years, like an undigested meal in my spiritual stomach.

Responsibility for God's earth is a tremendous task, as prophets of Israel had long pointed out. But some people of Jesus' time (even as today) had wearied of the Divine challenge, content to live for the moment only and ignore the future. Yet others, though also weary, continued to reach out to satisfy spiritual hunger by devoutly following the law of Moses. Then a humble man of Nazareth began to espouse a new religious thought—"Love thy neighbor...Do good to them that hate you...Wash the feet of your brother...Forgive the sinner..." But, because such teachings were at odds with the accepted formulations of the organized religious community of that day, a crucifixion followed which ended the ministry of the humble Carpenter. Now a new religious philosophy began to take form which crystallized, finally, in the didactic phrases of the Gospel of John. Thus people discovered, and quickly accepted, this religion which released man from the burden of struggling with the development of this world. For Jesus now said to them, as retold by John:

"My kingdom is not of this world... salvation is a free gift from God which cannot be earned by good works...I am the way, none entereth unto the Father except by me..."

And thus, teachings of the Carpenter—a universal love that knew neither creed nor sect—became distorted by his disciples into a dogmatic Christian theology which was a cop-out from man's responsibility for this planet earth. The Christian doctrine, as absolutist as the Jewish philosophy it proposed to supplant, declared that good works here would avail man nothing; God's Kingdom was not of this world.

I looked again at the wreckage about me and shook my head. Small wonder that two world wars had been waged by nations calling themselves Christian. For all their thousands of churches they had been unable to produce leadership strong enough to wipe out the causes of war. I walked to my waiting jeep and the regimental convoy moved out.

We were heading south now through many small towns, the neatness of the countryside attesting to the thrift of the German farmers. The contrast with the less-than-tidy farms of the French, in Alsace where we had first started fighting, was so obvious one of my men had said, "Hey, Captain, these German homes are clean! What are we fighting them for?" To which I had replied that we weren't fighting people, we were fighting government.

One afternoon we hit a winding stretch of road through beautiful countryside. Then, with a shock that actually made us jump, we discovered hundreds of dead horses, still harnessed to heavy guns. The carnage extended for over a mile. A retreating German artillery column had been strafed from the air, killing every living thing. But already allied bulldozer-tanks had cleared the way by pushing the carcasses right and left off the road. I shuddered. To farmer, or an animal lover, it was a jolt not easily erased from our memories.

In the last days of the war I walked, one night, into a confrontation with God on the scourge of war and the colossal waste of life with which it plagues this planet. In April of 1945 our Allied troops were rolling back the Nazi war machine toward what we expected might very well be a desperate "last stand" in the Bavarian Alps. Advance units of our 42d Division had blitzed into Munich with the mission of liberating the prisoners of the Nazi concentration camp at Dachua. I was with the main elements of our division, moving rapidly to linkup with them at Munich.

As night fell the roads over which our troops were approaching the city became clogged with military vehicles—trucks, jeeps, armored personnel carriers and artillery. I was in the lead jeep of our regimental headquarters company convoy when we reached a principal road junction into which several roads were funneling a mass of other military units. Here each driver was striving to insert his vehicle into the main road leading to Munich, some seven or eight miles to the south. The night was especially dark and complete black-out required of all military vehicles only added to the confusion. Vehicles from behind were moving out into the muddy fields, attempting to bypass the stymied vehicles, thus creating a hopeless tangle around the crossroad junction.

I had my jeep pull off the road and instructed the driver to wait for me. With my dark-lens flashlight showing only its half-by-one-inch strip of blue light (similar to the cat's-eyes lights on the vehicles), I moved to the road junction, took command of the situation and proceeded to unsnarl the traffic. Soon the stalled convoys began to move again.

It must have been all of an hour before the last vehicle of the many units cleared the crossroads and their cat's-eye taillights disappeared into the dusty darkness. Walking back to the spot where I had left my jeep I was startled to discover it gone. I searched the area. Nothing, no jeep, not another vehicle anywhere. I was alone in the night; alone in strange, battle-torn territory. In retrospect the situation was almost amusing, but at the time I was furiously angry.

Unslinging my carbine, I snapped a round into the chamber. Then, holding the light rifle at high-port-ready, I started down the dark road which led, I hoped, toward Munich. Occasionally I would pause, listen for footfalls, but hearing none, and seeing no flicker of light to mark whatever house or building I was passing, I kept on walking, ever alert, my finger on the carbine's trigger.

The overcast was gradually lifting, and one or two stars blinked in the darkness above me. I smiled inwardly, when I noticed them, my thoughts carried back to that earlier time in my life when I had hiked through the night in the Michigan forest—the night when I had first begun to talk with God. I remembered that those were the days, immediately after World War I—the war to end all wars, as we had thought of it then. Now, a scant 23 years later I was, myself, fighting in another world conflict, dedicated to that same high hope—the same elusive hope:

"Why is it, Lord?" I flung the question toward the stars at which my carbine threateningly pointed. "Why is it that we must snuff out so many lives, lay such shattering devastation upon this beautiful planet which you have created? Why do You permit this needless waste?"

"Why do I permit?" The answering voice of the Creator came not from above me this time, but in gentle tones. Close to my ear, as from a companion walking beside me through the night.

"Have you forgotten, my son, what you so recently discovered, that I have promised man absolute free will upon this planet? I cannot, therefore, go back upon my word. To pull his chestnuts out of the fire would be to take back from man his responsibility for the development of this world. It is the task I have entrusted to him, and for the accomplishment of which I have given him that power of free will. You see the logic, don't you?"

Again, as I had discovered before, God's reasoning was clarion clear, and it challenged me to think. I trudged on for a while, mulling it over before replying.

"All right, Lord," I finally countered, "then from that premise should I assume that you did not create man merely as a puppet, to people a capricious king's garden but, rather, as a creature with infinite potential, designed to work with you, God, in the ongoing evolution of this universe. Is that the Divine plan?"

"Intelligent analysis," agreed the Voice close to my ear.

"But what then, Lord, happens to those whose lives are cut short in battle? I can understand the responsibility, which you suggest is ours, for the ongoing progress of this earth. But, since You have not entrusted us, as yet, with knowledge of the continuation of that evolution, beyond the gateway of death, should we not know at least the destiny of those who must exit before they have had an opportunity to make their full contribution to this moment of eternity? Logic tells me we must develop that insight in order to achieve proper perspective.

"Clear-headed perception. And where would you look for such knowledge?"

"That's what I'm asking of You, Lord."

"But if I tell you, outright, you still will not understand, because you must discover it for yourself. That is the essence of the law, as you have already learned."

Once more the Lord was placing the challenge right back in my lap. I slowed momentarily, my boots impatient in the soft dust of the unfamiliar road, my troubled spirit reaching out into the darkness on either side of me—for suddenly I was no longer alone.

Shadowy figures of the men who had been killed while I led them now moved along with me: Sergeant Reiger, shot in the early hours of Christmas Eve, when we first took up positions on the Rhine River; Lieutenant Laye, blown apart by a mortar round in his foxhole in the Sessenheim Wood, and Private Peeler, who also gave his life in that battle. Other men were there too, privates, noncoms and officers of Company K and Regimental Headquarters Company. Even Charles Hutchinson, my close Infantry School buddy whom I had brought to the Rainbow Division with me, but who, impatient for combat duty had, before we left the States, transferred out of the 42d to become a replacement in the ETO, and there he was killed by an artillery shell as the Allied invasion pushed on beyond Omaha Beach.

Now, once again, these brave men were shoulder to shoulder beside me. We were marching together down a strange Bavarian road, and I was challenging the night sky for the attention of the Creator of the universe, seeking to wrest from him the answers to a soldier's destiny.

Still frustrated with the unresolved debate, I chided myself: "Keep moving, Jonesy. You can't resolve the eternal enigma of Divine purpose in one instant. Your own purpose, as of this moment, is to rejoin these two hundred other soldiers whose lives still depend upon your leadership."

I increased my pace. Another dog barked, close at hand. I swung my carbine in its direction, but kept on moving through the dark, my body instinctively answering to the messages from my feet—soft dirt and ruts, safe center of road, yielding grass, road's edge, move back. Unconsciously I was responding to the years of military training in nighttime operations which now, sharpened by battlefield application, had left me completely at home when moving over strange terrain in the dark. And so, tonight, except when barking dogs warned of human presence producing a chill to raise the hair on the nape of my neck, I tramped along, quite paradoxically drawing a quixotic pleasure from the smells and sounds of field and forest rising out of the night.

Yet somehow, as I moved resolutely along, my mind refused to let go of the argument with God. The silent

presence of fallen comrades nudged me and once more
I hurled an angry question into the darkness:

"Of what use then, Lord, are prayers for peace? In faith we
have petitioned You, but now You tell me it is impossible for
the powers of heaven to intervene. What purpose, then does
faith serve if we cannot pray to stop this useless waste of
lives?"

*"My son, I did not say, 'don't pray,' for that effort is man's
most powerful avenue of communication. I only challenge you
to apply logic to your prayers."*

"But, if we should not pray for peace?"

*"Ask yourself, what is peace? Does it fall, like rain from the
heavens?"*

"Of course not, Lord. Peace is a condition, not a product,
the peace we are asking for is the absence of armed conflict
between nations."

*"Now you are getting somewhere, my son. And how could
that be obtained?"*

"Why obviously, by eliminating the causes of war?"

*"Exactly. And from that point you have a logical basis on
which to construct prayers for that peaceful condition."*

"I begin to see. So, if I pray Lord help us..."

"Why us?" The Lord's tone was challenging.

"All right, me. Lord help me...find ways...to eradicate the
causes of war, is that better?"

*"Not only better, but entirely workable within the frame-
work of the law that governs the universe...the principle which
ordains non-interference in man's use of free will to act as his
mind may dictate. Therefore he must live with and bear responsibility for the results of his decisions—even his failure to
make them when so confronted with that need. It is the only
logical way to support absolute free will. He may not pray for
miracles to correct his mistakes, yet he can pray for inspira-*

*tion, for guidance, but he alone will have to make the decision
to use or to ignore it."*
"The Divine Gauntlet again?"
"You find that philosophical viewpoint helpful?"
"I like it, Lord. It puts responsibility on the individual, gives
purpose to human endeavor, which brings me back to my men
who were killed. Please show me, Lord, what purpose was
served by their violent removal from the task of developing
this planet..."

I never completed the dialogue, for at that moment
my eyes caught sight of a tiny flick of blue light in the
darkness ahead of me. On the instant I brought my
carbine into line with it and slowed my steps to control
their sound, realizing even as I did so that the dirt road
beneath me had become paved and I could discern the
shapes of houses close at hand. I was entering a town.

As I got closer the slip of blue became a vehicle's
tail light, switched off as I watched. I advanced carefully, and saw that it had joined a shadowy line of
American jeeps parked along the street. Moving closer
I discovered the markings on the vehicles identified
them as our own regimental train. I approached a dark
house near the curb. From the shadows of the porch an
unseen guard challenged me. I gave the password and
was quickly inside where I found the men of our regimental headquarters.

After explaining my absence to the adjutant I went in
search of my jeep driver and found him drinking coffee
with other soldiers. He looked up, startled, both relief
and worry in his eyes.

"What happened?" I asked crisply. "Didn't I tell you to wait
for me?"
"I didn't see you anywhere, Sir. I thought you had gone on

with the last vehicles. I didn't know where we were and I was
afraid —"

The dressing-down I'd planned to give him died in
my throat. Fear is ever present with front line troops—
you live with it, while trying to deny its presence—I'd
felt it, anew, as I started my lone walk from the crossroads. Now I looked into the troubled eyes of my
driver, and realized that somehow I had failed to inspire in this soldier that confidence which overrides
fear. I turned away and left him to his coffee and his
thoughts. I would have to do better in the future.

The next day we received orders from the division
commander informing us that all troops should visit
Dachau to see at first hand the unbelievable horrors
that man had unleashed upon his fellow man. So, I
sent most of our headquarters company that day, with
my executive officer in charge. The remaining men
would carry on the necessary functions of the company
and I would go with them to the concentration camp
the next day.

Later that morning, one of my MP platoon soldiers
came for me hurriedly.

"Captain, you'd better come. Down the street there's a
bunch of men with clubs. They're wearing prison clothes and
trying to break into a house."

I signaled several other soldiers to follow me and we
set off at the double with the MP. As we turned a corner of the residential street we saw the group. There
were maybe 15 or 20 men clustered around the entrance to a garage at the rear of a house. They had
already opened the garage door and were busily haul-

ing out large sacks of something. As we came closer one of the men left the group and came forward to meet us. He stopped in front of me. The dirty white and black striped prison garb he wore was torn and ill fitting but his face, through a ragged beard, was smiling. He gave me a half salute and spoke in English.

"Captain," he said, "We were sent out from Dachau to bring in food. We were told there was flour stored in this garage. Is it all right for us to take it?"

I looked at the men, their prison uniforms loose on bony figures, hollow eyes watching me from cavernous faces as they stopped piling the flour sacks on the several hand push carts they had brought with them. I glanced toward the house where from behind curtains two well-fed faces looked out in fear. Is it all right? The tragedy and the pathetic humor of the situation made me wince.

"Go ahead," I told them. "Take all you want."

The leader of the prisoners gave the signal and they eagerly resumed loading the sacks on their carts which were soon filled and they took off down the street. The leader turned back to wave his thanks and called out: "God bless you, sir."

Not me, I thought, you mean God bless the men who gave their lives that some of us might live to get here and put an end to the horror of those extermination camps.

And horror it was of the most unbelievable kind, I learned from the men of our company when they returned later that day. Some of the men were so emotionally thunderstruck by what they had seen that they could only shake their heads in disbelief and their voices choked when they tried to describe it. But others were more in control of themselves and they gave brief, harsh descriptions:

"Captain, you won't want to believe what you're going to see. And take a good grip on your stomach when you go in or you'll throw up. Some us did. It wasn't just the stench, Captain..."

"No, it was the naked, starved bodies, stacked up by those furnaces...

"And the terror on the faces of the dead ones in the box cars...Piled one on top of another they had been shot many times...And...and they found some still alive under the dead ones, covered with blood and vomit; God, they looked awful..."

"We've seen plenty of death in this war, Captain, but nothing like this—nothing. You'll see for yourself..."

But I did not get a chance to see first hand, because the next day our unit was on the move again. However, I saw the photographs that were printed in *The Stars and Stripes,* some of which were later relayed to the press back home. They were just as our men had reported to us: box cars loaded with starved human beings, some discovered still alive under the bodies of their fellow prisoners, who had been machine-gunned down by S.S. troopers before they fled in the face of advancing Allied armies. And, stacked like cordwood beside the grim furnaces were naked skeletal bodies waiting the fires which would remove forever, the evidence of this colossal genocide.

Citizens back home were to ask in disbelief for years to come, "Was it really that hideous? Were not some of those pictures staged, or retouched just to shock us?"

Today, as passing years have dimmed memory, and reduced the number of those who could witness to the truth, far too many young people, born since those terrible times, seem inclined to doubt that it ever actually happened. But our soldiers knew that the horror was more intense than any pictures could convey. There is something about a mass of naked bodies which cuts through all manmade pretensions! The piles of inhumanly abused bodies at Dachau declared the total moral depravity to which some of our fellowmen had descended. We who saw, at first hand, shall never forget.

Among ourselves we asked the question, how could human beings sink so low? We found no ready answers. Yet we were not smug about killing. We had been engaged in total warfare, the product of which is not pretty. There is no glory in snuffing out lives. Though as soldiers we were taking the lives of other soldiers, armed and bent on killing us, we had undertaken the unpleasant task only because we believe all men are entitled to live with human dignity, and our leaders, somehow, had been unable to ensure this right by peaceful deliberations. So the job fell to us, the average citizens. We put on the uniform, yet we treated the enemy with respect for his humanity. We nursed his wounded, fed and housed his prisoners of war, and gave respectful burial to his dead. Our purpose was not his obliteration but the suspension of his terrorism.

But German SS troops, on orders of leaders high in the government of the Third Reich, had taken unarmed people—men, women, and children—starved and brutalized them, then burned their bodies, so that not even bones would remain to tell future generations they had existed. It was the ultimate degradation that mankind could inflict upon himself. The experience at Dachau was, for many of us, the most somber of the war. Now we knew, for sure, we had been right in declaring war on such inhumanity.

The next day, with orders to continue pursuit of the retreating German Army, our Division drove on toward the Austrian border. Moving through the bombed out rubble of downtown Munich we passed long columns of German soldiers, their hands clasped above their heads in grim surrender. White flags hung from every window—sheets, tablecloths, anything white was used. It appeared that the armies of the Third Reich were finished. The lust for power which had plunged our world into its most devastating conflict was losing its drive. Now the peace, about which I had been debating with God only the night before, seemed near at hand.

I rode the lead jeep of our Regimental Headquarters convoy, as I had been doing every day since we began the push through Germany. Sitting sideways on the folded camouflage net (placed across the hood) I could observe the vehicles behind me as well as the road before us. My carbine was at the ready in my right hand, the butt resting against my lap. The day was cloudy gray, as had been so very many of the days both in France and Germany. But the cheerless atmosphere did not hold down our spirits, for spring was at hand and despite the chill we received from Dachau, evidence of the war's end became more convincing with every mile. A small group of German soldiers with their hands raised in surrender came out of the woods. With our thumbs, we pointed them to the rear and kept on moving. The MPs would pick them up; POWs were not our task now.

Main elements of the German First Army were ahead of us. Division intelligence had reported they had the capability to make a last desperate stand from a redoubt in the Austrian Alps. Toward the possibility they might even use gas, our regimental S-4 had kept several truckloads of gas masks following close to the forward elements of our troops. Now our Division was moving purposefully south, all attention focused on that ragged mountain line on our horizon.

Our headquarters vehicles paused at a crossroads to check maps with the road net. On the signposts were directions to Salzburg, Garmich Partenkirchen, Innsbruck, Tittmoning and Zurich. Between the signs was a wayside shrine, a fairly common sight in Bavaria. The shrine had been freshly decorated with green boughs and a few flowers, though where such blooms were secured in that bleak, war-torn countryside was something to ponder. But their presence was a visual reminder of man's eternal need to satisfy spiritual hunger.

We took the fork marked Tittmoning and a few hours later arrived at that same small town on the Austrian border. We established the regimental command post in an empty building and wire crews moved out to make contact with the battalions who already had patrols probing into the Alpine foothills. Forward movement of the Division now paused and we spent several days in Tittmoning.

Then, one night, I was walking down the dark street, from the CP to our POW cage on the edge of town, when suddenly, from a line of parked trucks, headlights blazed forth to illuminate the entire area. Instantly I rushed toward the vehicles.

"Put those lights out, soldier," I shouted. "Do you want the Jerry to strafe us? Get em out! Get em out!" But the headlights did not go out and one of the drivers called back "It's OK, Captain. The war is over! We just heard it on the radio. It's over, the war's over!"

"Well, you put those lights out until we get orders from headquarters, you hear? It could be a trick. I'll let you know as soon as it's official."

Reluctantly, one by one, the truck headlights were extinguished and the night resumed the total blackness with which we had become so familiar. I headed back for the CP to check with our communications platoon. They kept tuned in to the Division net. Other staff officers were already there. Yes, civilian radio was active, broadcasting that the German high command had surrendered, but no military orders were out yet, so the regimental commander told us to play safe. "Keep all lights out, for tonight, and maintain full security. Tomorrow we'll know for sure."

I went back to the company area, relayed the colonel's orders, then stood in the dark street and looked up. Once more, stars were in command of the sky and with a start I suddenly realized there was a unique relationship between those distant heavenly bodies and the

event about to take place on this night-shaded portion
of planet earth. Again, communication with the Creator
stirred within me:

"All right, God, so Your heavenly lights never went out, did
they? Through all these long years of unhappy nights, while
our struggles have blacked out the lights over many continents
of this globe, Yours have stayed on. You never retreated. You
never covered up in the face of aerial bombing. You let us go
ahead and fight for what we believe in. Though we've literally
torn this planet apart, You've kept the sun shining and the
rains pouring down to bless us, with no partiality toward either
side. Now our lights are going on again all over the world, as
the song tells it, and your everlasting challenge is facing us
again—isn't it Lord—make this world a better place than you
found it. That's right isn't it?" Through the silent night a soft
wind was blowing, and matching it, within my mind, the voice
of God pressed gently upon my consciousness.
     "Do you accept it, then, my son?"
     "The Divine Gauntlet? Yes, Lord. For myself I must. I can-
not speak for the others."
     *"But, yes, you can. You've been wrangling with Me in the
name of those men whom you led, demanding answers as to
why they left a task here uncompleted. Your concern has
bought their unfinished task. Your privilege is doubled, com-
pounded now, because you worked together, cared together
and together reached beyond yourselves."*
     "But why, Lord, were they not allowed to finish?"
     *"Have you not learned? In evolution nothing is ever fin-
ished. It's the contribution of the instant that counts, that carries evolution forward. There is no cessation of movement.
What appears as still and serene is merely a reflection of the
beauty of accomplishment, observed in the instant of creating
its moment of eternity. And so each moment provides its own,
fresh inspiration to the challenge of the next."*
     "But they were such good men, Lord. Why couldn't they
have gone on creating those moments?"

"And so they shall. Do you think I have no plan beyond this planet?" The voice of God grew angry. *"Good or bad, in your view, do you think I have not loved them, watched with joy and pain every moment, as their personalities developed under the challenges of this world's unfolding? Do you think I cannot use those souls, now, in continuing that evolution elsewhere?"*

"Do you mean, Lord, you will not hold them in limbo, or purgatory, whatever or wherever or whenever, until judgment day?"

"Is it logical my son?" Once more God's voice was gentle, patient. *"Is it logical that souls should wait, unused, in some celestial closet while the universe spins on its evolutionary way? There is no logic in that. It's time to look beyond the limit of man's earlier spiritual horizon. As for judgment, that accrues to man in the instant of his actions, to be modified or increased by his succeeding behavior. So that when he leaves this stage, whether at end of a normal life, or suddenly in battle, like your buddies, (or those called your enemies) or in violent death from accident, or in payment for committing murder, his soul has already been started on its next evolutionary cycle. Death is merely the door to that next sequence. There is no standing still."*

But if they are moving on, Lord, will we ever meet again?"

"That depends on how strong has been the bond which drew you together." The voice of God was like a cello playing against the soft night wind. *"Love is the universal law drawing souls together. Like the force of gravity which binds the earth's mountains to itself, love's power is infinite."*

I glanced up again at the visible stars, each holding its precise place in the immensity of our galaxy, and I knew our individual lives, however insignificant they might appear to us at times, were a calculated part of God's evolving universe and therein lay the purpose for our being here.

With confirmation of the German surrender our Division was ordered into Austria as occupation troops.

When we moved forward now, we traveled for the first time on the "Autobahn," that superb concrete, divided highway which the Germans had built to connect their principal cities. Of course, our Allied air force bombers had destroyed every bridge and overpass, thus denying use of the broad concrete strips to vehicular use without time-consuming detours. Some of these detours we now negotiated on the stretch of Autobahn which linked Munich to Salzburg. I am certain that the efficiency of this road net had made a lasting impression on General Eisenhower for later, when "Ike" became president, one of the outstanding achievements of his administration was the launching of our own "Autobahn," today's magnificent Interstate Highway System.

Now, as our troops traveled the Autobahn, they found that detours around the blown-up bridges allowed our soldiers to examine the densely planted evergreen forests that lined both sides of the Autobahn. Here in the wide aisles between the orderly planted rows of trees we found, to our surprise, great numbers of partially assembled airplane fuselages. The cockpit canopies were made of plexiglass, which some of our men were quick to rip out and cut up into souvenirs, while others tore out the yards of electric wiring and fixtures that lined the cockpits. What they intended to do with these was not clear, but they were souvenirs of the war and Americans are great collectors of mementos.

The next day it was raining hard as we stopped in a small Bavarian town. Our headquarters company took over, for noon mess, a large empty house on the corner of a block. The army range had been set up in the kitchen and the men, with their full mess kits, were sitting around on the floor of the downstairs rooms, eating, when I came in.

"We've set up a tent fly in the garden for your officers," the mess sergeant told me, "with benches and a table of sorts. It's dry if not luxurious."

I thanked the sergeant, took out my canteen cup and moved to get my own meal when two men appeared at the kitchen door and asked for the commanding officer. As I turned to meet them I noticed that they were wearing OD trousers and Eisenhower jackets, without any identifying insignia on sleeves or breast pockets, and the uniforms were quite reputably clean. I said hello.

"I'm Captain Jones. What can I do for you?"

One of the pair introduced himself as a war correspondent, (whose name I can't recall now) and could they possibly scrounge a meal off us?

"Surely, with pleasure," I told them and turned to the mess sergeant who responded with:

"Captain, we lost our officer's mess gear sometime back. But we'll improvise, Sir, if these men don't mind makeshift tableware."

So, with can lids for plates, one canteen cup and a tomato can for their coffee, we took our guests out into the rain soaked garden and, ducking under the tent fly, sat down at the improvised table.

The war correspondent was gracious in his appreciation of our impromptu hospitality, though he did not volunteer the name of his companion who had sat down next to me. As we ate I kept glancing sideways at

his profile, which seemed vaguely familiar. Finally it
came to me and I asked him:

"Aren't you Colonel Lindbergh?"

The modest smile he returned in acknowledgment was
the same self-effacing grin I remembered from 18 years
before. I told him I had run alongside of his open
touring car, in Central Park, at the end of the welcome-
home parade with which New York City had greeted Charles
Lindberg's return from his famous solo trans-Atlantic flight.

Colonel Lindbergh then explained to us that he was
on a special government assignment to assess the progress in German development of a new airplane en-
gine, the jet. Actually, said Lindbergh, they already
had test models in the sky, and it was his opinion that
if the Germans had had six more months to complete
manufacture of a fleet of the jet planes, they would
have won the war.

"How could that have been?" I wanted to know.
"Because," replied Lindbergh, "we had nothing in our pro-
peller-driven Air Force that could even begin to compete with
jets for speed. Jet bombers would flash in over our positions
and be gone before we could engage them."
Then I told Colonel Lindbergh of the hundreds of partially
assembled fuselages we had found in the forests lining the
Autobahn.
"I've seen them," said Lindbergh "they were jets."

The colonel explained that our saturation bombing
of Germany's industrial centers had so destroyed their
factories that they had been forced to seek new working areas. The evergreen forests of Bavaria offered
good camouflage for the assembly of planes, with the

special advantage of ready-made takeoff strips. The Autobahn's miles-long stretches of concrete between the bombed bridges provided ideal runways for the launching of jet planes. Yet, in spite of this ingenious adaptation to crisis, Germany had been unable to rebuild its bombed factories fast enough to provide the parts necessary to complete the jets. Our Allied air force's "strategic bombing," deep behind enemy lines, had truly shortened the war.

I don't know whatever happened to Colonel Lindbergh's report to the government. Maybe it never went beyond some department in the Pentagon. But surely it must never have reached the attention of the president and Congress or those same civilian leaders, just five years later, would not have been so quick to deny the use of "strategic bombing" to General MacArthur in Korea.

The next day we moved deeper into Austria, assigned to supervise demobilization of the German First Army which had deployed itself in the mountains of the Tyrol. Our division headquarters was at Kitzbuhl and our 232d Regiment set up in St. Johan, which was also headquarters for the German First Army.

As headquarters commandant, one of my responsibilities was to provide the holding compounds for POWs captured by the regiment as we advanced.

My last POW cage had been in Tittmoning, where we held many thousands of German troops on the final day of hostilities. Our security platoon sergeants had proved very resourceful in handling that exceptionally large mass of enemy soldiers. They simply turned over to the German officers the job of organizing the jumble of prisoners into an orderly camp—which they did speedily and efficiently, leaving our security platoon free to provide guards and food. But the guards had no problems because the Germans were weary of fighting, they realized the end was at hand, and they knew they would be treated better by American troops than by the Russians.

This attitude of distrust for the Russians was voiced very clearly to us by many German officers we talked with in the Tyrol those first days after the surrender. They told us the Russians were not to be trusted, that they would turn against the Allies, because the socialist philosophy would never work in cooperation with nations of the free world.

> "You will have to fight the Russians in the end," said one German officer to me, "so you had better do it now. And we're ready to help you."

Having had no personal contact, yet, with the Soviets I was reluctant to believe this of our supposed Allies, and told the Germans so. But the German officers knew better and warned us to keep our eyes open. The Soviets would turn against us, as indeed they surely did. And it wasn't long before I saw for myself the brutality of the communist state in action.

At the request of my general, I volunteered to remain on duty for two years with the Occupation Forces. I became part of G-2, the division intelligence section. In this capacity I came in close contact with the work of resettling thousands of refugees who, like chaff before the winds of war, had moved from place to place across the European continent. Now they were gathered in camps, preparatory to being returned to their native homelands.

But most refugees from the countries of the Soviet Union did not want to return. Life under communist rule had become unbearable to them. They refused to board the trains which would take them back. They begged for political asylum, anything that would let them live away from Soviet rule. There was much haranguing about this at the top levels of the Allied governments. The Soviets insisted that the refugees must be sent home to them. The American, British and French finally capitulated to the Soviet demands, and orders came down to our refugee camps in Austria to put the refugees on the trains, forcefully if need be, that they must go back to Russia. The terror and horror that resulted was pitiful to behold. Many refugees committed suicide rather than go; others fought and wept as the trainload of locked cars left Austria for the Soviet border.

Allied civilian personnel in charge of the refugee camp, and we, the military personnel who were responsible for security of the territory, were saddened by this decision of our Allied governments and carried out their orders with great reluctance. The situation demonstrated the tragedy which results when civilian officials in high places of power, with the best of intentions, but physically far removed from the area of activity concerned, make arbitrary decisions about the personal freedom of individual citizens whom they have never met, and on whose territory they have never walked. I thought at the time, here we are creating a climate in which the seeds of future wars will surely germinate. And I remembered my discourse with God on praying for peace—yes, here, indeed, was an area in which to focus prayer and personal effort—for the next battle to make peace a lasting condition on this planet had already begun.

In the military we have a rule for success in combat operations which says: "Nothing takes the place of personal reconnaissance." When officers train, the phrase is repeatedly dinned into their subconscious: "Personal reconnaissance, Lieutenant, personal reconnaissance". I believe that today we could very well pass that rule on to our civilian leaders at all levels of government, urging them to "Make personal reconnaissance, a habit— get out and talk with the people, get out and walk over the terrain, before you make decisions about other people's lives." The rule applies equally well to business, industry, education, and yes, even religion. On that score I observed that the Carpenter of Nazareth, the Buddah and the Chinese teacher Confucius were all leaders who recognized the value of on-the-spot personal reconnaissance among the people.

For the next few months, as I worked with the occupation forces on demobilization of the German war machine, I watched favorable conditions for future conflict being brewed in the kettles of disarmament. I saw evidence of the roots of war still growing underneath the now quiet fields and city streets as man, released from the challenges of titanic conflict, began walking, with his guard down, into the deceptive calm of peace. It distressed me to see trends developing among our own as well as former enemy personnel, which were like warning flags—patterns of greed—greed for more power, more possessions, more acclaim. This was the time, I thought, for concerned persons to be praying for God's guidance. Now was the time to be searching for ways to eliminate those potential causes of war. But I found no clergy leading us in that direction.

I think I really began to pray earnestly about it myself, on the day I was privileged to attend the first Jewish religious service to be held in Austria since before Hitler began their destruction. It was the summer of 1946. My wife, Ginny, had joined me in Salzburg that May, coming over with the initial group of families authorized to join military personnel of the occupation forces. For both of us it was our first attendance at a synagogue. Apart from the ritual which requires that men cover their heads and women seat themselves in a separate area of the house of worship, we found their manner of communication with God not radically different from our own, yet there was a difference; it showed in their faces. These were people who had suffered terribly. Their loved ones had been torn from them, tortured, gassed and burned, yet the strength of their faith in God seemed increased rather than decreased—they still found God's world good. Never had history recorded a more impressive demonstration of the faith of Job. Ginny and I were profoundly stirred as we stood, side by side, with these devout people, raising our voices together in prayer and song.

Recalling my months of close association with the Jewish people during the New York run of *The Eternal Road,* and my own small part in the liberation of the Dachau concentration camp, I felt a deep spiritual kinship with these people. The God of Abraham, Isaac, and Jacob, the God who met Moses on Mt. Sinai, was as real to me in that historic service as when I had been talking with Him on the road to Munich, beside my campfire in the peaks above Yosemite, and in the wings of the theatre during the last act of Cyrano. Now, as the rabbi led us in a prayer of thanks for deliverance from our enemies, I knew at last who the enemy really was.

For the enemy is not a nation or a race of people, nor even individual humans who may commit acts of violence upon us, because all of mankind are brothers, and brothers must not be enemies. The actual enemy of mankind lurks in traits of character which humans allow to develop within themselves—thus destroying their ability to love and to be loved. The playwright Rostand had pointed this out in the last act of *Cyrano de Bergerac*. In that scene the heroic Cyrano is dying from an assassin's attack. In the final moment he stands, with sword out, defiant, his back to the tree, striking out at what he calls his ancient enemies—Pride, Prejudice, Envy, Cowardice, Vanity.

Thus did Cyrano enumerate what for him were the worst enemies of society. I, myself, would add two more villains to the list—Greed and Lust for Power. I believe these seven are the evil sources from which armed conflict eventually springs. They are true enemies of mankind. They are the real foes against whom to marshal our efforts for peace. For myself this means that wherever I observe these enemies operating within the scope of my own life's activities, I must pray for courage and work diligently toward eliminating these basic causes of war.

CHAPTER V

The Guidepost Years:

Spiritual Discoveries Of A Father,
A Farmer, An Editor

 y wife and I returned to the United States in April of 1947, our minds and hearts set on two goals—we wanted to work, in some way, toward maintaining universal peace, and we wanted passionately to raise a family.

In the matter of children we had had, thus far, no success. While still in Austria we were counseled by an army physician. He had been a gynecologist before being called up for military service, so when the military wives began arriving he was delighted to return to his specialty and headed up the newly created maternity section in our Salzburg military hospital. Twice he sent Ginny to the hospital in Munich for treatment. On the second visit I was waiting in an outer office and overheard two medical corpsmen discussing Ginny's condition. Said the one, "That major is out of luck, his wife just isn't going to have any babies." The statement hit me like a blow to the stomach. They didn't know of course, that I could ·hear them. I said nothing, and never told Ginny about it till years later.

153

On August 16, 1947, I finally received my separation from active duty, and at the same time was sworn
in again as a member of the Army Officer's Active
Reserve Corps. To those friends who asked why I had
volunteered for this peace time military responsibility I
replied that I didn't believe the hostilities were truly
over. I felt we would be needed again, probably within
five years. As it turned out the Korean War broke out
in three.

My intuition in this matter was the result of what I
observed while still in the occupation forces, in Austria, and I almost stayed in the service because of it.
Soon after the Japanese surrender General Collins had
offered me a commission in the Regular Army. I said
I'd think it over. A short time later I was acting as
commandant of our Rainbow University when he
brought it up again.

Rainbow U. was part of the Army's plan to provide
college level courses in academic subjects for the occupation troops stationed throughout Europe. The schools
were a unique experiment that gave American soldiers
a chance, while still on duty, to begin their return to
civilian life. Our Rainbow U., located in a picturesque
alpine village of the Tyrol, offered two-year college
studies in liberal arts and technological subjects. Our
teachers, drawn from enlisted and officers ranks, were
chosen for experience and knowledge of the subject.
We had a particularly talented group of "professors."
These resourceful soldiers scoured the countryside for
equipment and local help. The results provided the students an electronics lab with facilities that would have
been a credit to MIT. The geology students made an

expedition to the Paisterze Glacier. The forestry students worked with local foresters in a centuries-old mountainside tree farm. The classes in languages, business law, economics and the other 25 scholastic subjects, all benefited from this cooperation with the friendly Austrian population.

But for me the most exciting part of the whole school program had been the counseling sessions, in which we would help each new matriculating group of 400 students choose studies to fit, or launch, their life's careers. I realized then how much young people needed the wisdom of experience to help channel their energy and talents. At Rainbow U. we encouraged the students to reach beyond themselves.

General Collins had come down to address the first graduating class. After lunch he once again asked me to accept a Regular Army commission. When I hesitated he asked:

"Starr, what do you actually want to do with your life?"

"Sir," I replied, in words that surprised myself, "I want to help influence public opinion towards making a better world."

"In that case," replied my general, "much as I hate to see you go, I can't ask you to remain with the Regular Army. A soldier's duties do not permit the same freedom to express personal opinions which you would have as a civilian."

So in that moment, as in the Indian leap I'd made from the improvised stage in the Commodore Hotel ballroom some twenty years before, a die was cast concerning my future.

And now, as Ginny and I stood in the California sunshine outside Post Headquarters building at Camp

Stoneman, I was again a civilian—just one more of the millions of American citizens who had walked through the yellow fog of war, and returned to the deceptive calm of peace. But I could still in the back reaches of my mind hear the eerie thudding of the Horses of the Apocalypse—I knew I would always hear them. And I knew too, that only in such constant awareness lay any hope of keeping sheathed the swords of war.

Feeling very much like adventurers about to undertake an expedition into the unknown, Ginny and I left the post and drove back to the motel. As I packed our belongings into the jeep I found myself continuing with God, our battlefield dialogue:

"All right, Lord, so it's finally over. Yes, I'm grateful that I survived, thankful for the insights you revealed to me, and for the challenges you laid before me. Please now, continue to walk with me as I face them. I don't know yet where the challenge will lead, and I will need answers as I search, but I accept the responsibility and I shall be listening for your voice."

I stowed the last bag behind our seats, climbed in and started the motor. Ginny smiled and patted my arm. "Where to, honey?" she asked. I adjusted the sun visor and squinted through the shimmering heat waves toward the horizon.

"I guess it's follow the Yellow Brick Road," I replied. "We are now embarking on that long delayed honeymoon-vacation. We've got four month's accumulated leave pay. We'll camp out in the mountains for a while; then, by easy stages work back east, visit your folks in Missouri and get to my old country home in New York this fall."

"You still want to farm?"

"I yearn to be close to the soil."

"And what about influencing public opinion, as you expressed it to General Collins?"

"I really don't know yet, but I believe God will show me a way?"

"I hope we'll know it when we see it."

"I hope so, too, dear," I replied heading the jeep towards the distant mountains.

The army jeep is certainly the most appropriate heir to the legacy of the horse. Like its four-legged ancestor it will go to almost any place man's pioneering imagination can conceive of reaching. On top of our own four-wheeled individual of this popular breed of gasoline mustang, a wooden body had been superimposed while it was still in Europe. It's shape was square and it lacked streamlining, but it was as rugged as the jeep itself.

In a few more days we had left the paved highways leading into the Sierras south of Yosemite, and were following an old trail that became more indistinct the farther we penetrated into the mountains. In places, the thread of the path led between outcroppings of rock over which the jeep lurched crazily. Finally the trail leveled out in a stretch of primeval forest along the edge of which flowed a sparkling stream.

When people think of "getting away from it all" they must dream of such an idyllic hideaway. We made camp.

For several days we relaxed here, marveling at the sheer beauty of this remote spot, and enjoying each other's company as never before in the three-plus years of our marriage. We cooked and slept, talked, planned dreams for the future, and dozed lazily in the mottled sunshine beneath the pine trees. We bathed in the snow-fed waters of the stream, gasping gleefully as we splashed the icy liquid against our bare bodies till we were exhausted from laughing.

On the morning of the fifth day we were still in our bedroll when we heard the sound of a motor car and looking up saw an auto flash by just a hundred yards away through the trees! A hasty reconnaissance in that direction disclosed a good paved highway cutting through the forest, its smooth surface hidden from our campsite's view by a low rise in the forest floor. Sheepishly we looked at each other—our supposed "hideaway" was as exposed as any ranger-policed public campground. The fact that no cars had passed that way for four days was a freak of happenstance.

In amused silence we prepared breakfast. We had not planned to leave our idyll for several days yet, but now the romantic charm of the place was broken—the spell of Camelot evaporated. We packed our gear, drove through the trees to the paved road, and headed the jeep generally eastward.

Nine and a half months later, back on the farm in New York, with crop fields planted and construction begun on a new home, our first son, Gregory Scott was born. Our cup of joy overflowed.

Greg was christened at our non-denominational Christ Church on Quaker Hill. His godmother was the actress I had once been engaged to, his godfather my old friend Lowell Thomas. Strange indeed, sometimes, are the threads that form the pattern of our lives.

By the time our second son, David, was born in March of 1950, I had my strawberry field well established and was growing tons of fancy tomatoes to meet heavy local market demands. At the same time I continued building on our new home which, because I wanted to do all the work myself, was progressing rather slowly. But I was happy. I loved working the fields, milking our family cow and building, room by room, our simple concrete-block farmhouse.

Then one day that spring, a dear friend came to see us. On the second day of his visit he came out to the field where I was weeding strawberries. Squatting down beside me Nathan launched into an oblique discourse on the subject of using one's talents. It was obvious he was aiming at me, so I started to defend my position:

"Look, my friend, I am by nature well suited to farming. It is an honest and necessary occupation. Actually I'm only responding to the blood of my pioneer ancestors."

"Sure, sure, I know," Nathan replied, "but I also know that the blood of chieftains, lawyers, and clergymen added their genes to the mixture that's in you. What about them?"

"So what?" I told him. "I'm me, I'm something else again. What do you want me to do?"

"Use all that's come down to you, Starr, that's what I'm driving at. Sure farming's important, but there are a hundred others who can do this job, and they can't do anything else. But you could do so much more than this. I'm not a particularly religious man, Starr, but I do believe God expects each of us to make the very most of our individual talents. And, when we waste them, it's not good for us. In fact there's something about that in Scriptures, if I could remember it."

That night I told Ginny about Nathan's sermon to me in the strawberry patch. I knew she agreed with his viewpoint, but she had never asked me to change. She had never nagged or importuned me. She was willing that I should decide the direction in which we moved our lives. I valued that loyalty and was concerned that I should not allow my will to smother her own. In the days following Nathan's visit, I made the subject a matter of earnest prayer, asking God for signs to guide me if my present career efforts were moving in the wrong direction. As so often happens, God's answer came through a chain of unexpected events.

A short time later I developed unusual back pains, which became increasingly severe within a few weeks. One day in the middle of summer, I was weeding a tomato field when my back literally froze up on me. I could not get to my feet. They rolled me onto an ambulance stretcher and I spent the next two weeks in a hospital with a low-back strain, diagnosed permanent.

This unexpected disability put an effective finish to the farm work I loved so much. The doctor suggested I hire help for the field labor and content myself with managing the farm. But the idea of giving up having my hands and feet in the soil did not appeal to me at all. If I had wanted to manage men I would have remained in the Army.

So, I set about rethinking my career occupation—and in the process came back to my impulse statement to General Collins, and my conversation with God on the night walk to Munich. What talents did I have that could work toward eliminating the causes of war? There are those who contend that hunger is a primary cause, why not work in that direction? But analysis told me that was not the answer. Hunger is a basic condition of man's existence, part of the challenge of living which God has built into the evolution of life, which each man must resolve for himself and those he loves. Also, satisfying hunger of the stomach is a very relative thing. The people in our prisons do not want for food, yet the majority of them are not less combative toward their fellow man. The real problem is removing the belligerence from these individuals, changing their mental attitudes.

Finally, I came to the conclusion that while men fought wars for the possession of physical things—land, food, property, people—yet things, themselves, were not the true cause of conflict. It was the attitude of man toward the physical possession (whether in greed or with love) that created conditions of war or peace. Therefore, it appeared to me, that if man would live in peace with his neighbor he must improve his frame of mind, his outlook on this very physical world—keeping in mind that this earth is the creation of God, whose only visible attribute to us, at this stage of our development, is that of spirit.

Such improvement of attitudes ought to be the primary purpose of all religions, it seemed to me. Yet it is not, and wars continue. Which is the reason I have felt a responsibility to keep in training with the Army Reserves. My country may need me again. Far too many religions have failed to reconcile spiritual values to the world's pragmatic needs.

The wisdom of Confucius and Lao Tzu set forth wonderfully practical recommendations for physical behavior between individual human beings, thus making for a far better world. Yet, for some inscrutable

reason, these Chinese masters ignored the spiritual element. While the teachings of Buddhism go to the other
extreme, stressing the value of right living in this
world, yet the Buddha challenged his followers to seek
union with the Spirit of Creation by withdrawing from
the world, through meditation. Surely a confusing con-
tradiction. Pre-dating both of these faiths, and still a
vital religion to millions, today, the multi-faceted
creeds of Hinduism cover a wide spectrum that ranges
from animism to asceticism, all centered around the
basic premise that life is a succession of birth and re-
birth, but without individual purpose in the process. To
the Hindu, the escape from this wheel of perpetual re-
incarnation is to merge one's spiritual self (one's soul)
with the eternal Brahman.

The other three great religions—Judaism, from which
Christianity was born, and Islam, which grew out of
both of these, have much in common which should
bind them together—they worship the one God, creator
of the universe, and believe in the universal brotherhood of man. However, what divides these wonderful
people are the methods (dogma and ritual) by which
their religions profess and practice those beliefs. Today, I see those unfortunate differences as a failure to
interpret God's purpose for man's existence on this
planet, in terms that stand up to logical, 20th century
thought processes.

The challenge for myself, then, was to find a career
field where my energies could be used to help my fellow men reconcile these physical and spiritual differences, in order that together we can make this world a
better place for those who will follow us. This line of

thinking led me to consider work fields dealing with public communication, areas which ironically I had in the past tried to avoid. Now, once again, I saw the professions of clergyman and journalist staring at me. The clergy was most easily discounted because it would require working within precise religious boundaries, and my conscience would not permit me to accept such limitations. This left the field of journalism—certainly broad and varied enough to provide scope for any viewpoint I might feel impelled to develop. Then, remembering the old maxim that whatever you hate will surely pursue you, I laughed at myself. Well, so be it. I would no longer avoid that challenge but meet it head on. If it were the right direction toward which to bend my efforts, then God would give me signs. Once more I turned to the Creator:

"All right, Lord," I said, "the summer's behind me, and so is farming. I'm going in to New York City and begin leaving resumes with publishing houses and employment offices specializing in the editorial field. But I'll be listening for your voice and hoping for a nudge."

And I did just that. I made the rounds of the publishers, like I'd made the rounds of theatrical producers 25 and 30 years before. I also went up to Columbia University where, under the GI Veteran's Bill, I signed up for journalism courses in their School of Continuing Adult Education: Newspaper Editing, Short Story Writing, Literature and Playwriting.

I have always believed in the philosophy which recommends that you pray as though everything depended on God, and work as though everything depended on yourself. By Christmas I was deep in my college courses, and I had some promises from several publishing houses, but no job, yet. However, I did have one offer, such are the contradictions of employment offices, from a picture gallery on East 57th Street, to become a sales executive on their gallery floor, representing contemporary and "Old Master" art to patrons of wealth and substance. I held off accepting, and made more rounds of the journalistic field.

Then on a foggy, wet day the Friday after Christmas, at the suggestion of my sister, I went to see the director of a small inspirational magazine called *Guideposts* which was being published on Quaker Hill, just three miles from our farm. The magazine's founder and publisher was Pinky Thornburg a long time friend of our family. Pinky (Mr. Raymond Thornburg, chairman of the board of the Pawling Rubber Company) was a man deeply concerned for the fabric of society. Immediately after World War II, at the same time that I was in Austria, distressed by the signs of future wars which I saw taking root underneath the recently deserted battlefields, Pinky was distressed by the signs of moral decay which he saw emerging here in America, as the country began retooling from a war to a peacetime economy. And Pinky (like Konosuko Matsushita, the head of Panasonic Industries in Japan, whose strangely parallel story I discovered in 1973) felt that business men were logical leaders to move the country forward, morally, as well as economically. Pinky told his story to me one day on the commuter train to New York.

"I decided," said Pinky, "that if businessmen were to lead, they needed something to provide them with inspiration and guidance. Now, if beside the *Kiplinger Letter* he had a weekly inspirational letter, something to raise his sights in the matter of ethics and moral values, the American businessman would be in a strong position to lead the country into a promising era of peace and progress.

"But what would be in that inspirational letter?" asked Pinky. "certainly not cliche phrases from other leaders, not preaching relayed from church pulpits, but something new and fresh. I would get businessmen to share experiences from their personal lives, stories which would demonstrate the practicality of applying spiritual values to meeting the problems of daily living. I asked several businessmen friends if they would open their personal lives to share such experiences. They were enthusiastic, and eagerly volunteered stories, Captain Eddie Rickenbacker, J.C. Penney and many others.

"So, thus encouraged," said Mr. Thornburg. "I started *Guideposts* as a weekly four-page, inspirational letter. Within a year we combined these into a monthly, of 24 pages, and *Guideposts* was born. Our dining room table became a litter of envelopes and mailing addresses, of personal letters and many others.

"But, at the start," said Pinky, "I began to think that, since we were dealing with people's religious experiences, I should have a clergyman on our editorial board, just to add a note of spiritual authority. I didn't want clergymen's stories, or preaching, or church dogma interpreted. I wanted *Guideposts* to be a lay man's publication, of, by and for the layman. People of every religious faith, or of no religious persuasion whatever, but people whose daily life experiences illustrated the use of, need for, or seeking toward spiritual values in solving life's problems. But, where to find a clergyman with such a broad viewpoint, or of such wide acceptance by the general public?

"I searched the field," said Pinky, "and narrowed the possibilities to three or four men. First I approached the Rev. Dr. Ralph Sockman, whose weekly radio program endeared him to millions. I asked Dr. Sockman to join me. But he was too heavily obligated, he said, to take on anything new. Certainly, *Guideposts* was new at that moment. In fact no other publication, then or since, has ever come out with such a broad, interfaith editorial policy. Well, I next went to see Norman Vincent Peale and invited him to join *Guideposts* as our spiritual advisor. He liked the idea and, with the enthusiasm that is his trademark, came into the *Guideposts* family and stayed with us."

I did not know all of this on that foggy day as I drove my jeep, through the mists, up Mizzentop Road. But I had an eerie feeling that God was watching over my shoulder.

Guideposts office was in a large, white mansion on the crest of a Berkshire ridge. The house had once been the home of Albert Akin one of the builders of the railroad that pierced the Harlem Valley to bring thousands of gallons of milk (and later thousands of commuters) to New York City. In the library heavy with beautiful oak carvings, I met with Fred Decker, *Guideposts* business manager:

"Strange you should come here today, Starr," he told me, "Only day before yesterday at a meeting of our executive committee staff, we decided to add two men to our editorial staff. We need an experienced editor to work directly under our executive editor. No, your resume, Starr, doesn't show enough experience for that job. But, our second man was to be someone who would begin at the bottom of the ladder, as it were. He'd be used for many jobs—running copy to the printer, researching at the library, maybe even doing some cub reporting. Of course we were visualizing a somewhat younger man, a college graduate, perhaps. Someone looking for experience."

I smiled at Fred's apparent discomfiture, and turned to look out the window. The fog was so dense I could barely see the outlines of my jeep.

"Tell me," I said. "What is your magazine trying to do?"

"Help people lead better lives," replied Fred.

Well, I thought, it's a bottom-of-the-ladder job all right, a sort of editorial go-fer, not a very challenging prospect. The magazine is only five years old, boasting a circulation of less than 200,000—but, when Fred said what they were trying to do, I thought I heard, ever so faintly, out there in the fog beyond my jeep, the sound of trumpets...

"I'll take the job," I said, turning back from the window, "if you'll give me a shot at it. I may not be a college graduate, though I'm attending Columbia right now, and I may not be as young as you visualized. Most college men are in their twenties, I'm already 45, but I'd guarantee you no younger man will cover as much ground as fast as myself. My Army buddies didn't nickname me Captain Double Time for nothing. And as for experience—let's just say, I've had plenty. Besides I believe in what you're trying to accomplish with the magazine."

Fred said the job was mine, if the executive editor approved me. He would telephone Mr. LeSourd to expect me for an interview, next Monday morning, at the editorial office in New York City.

I liked Len LeSourd the moment he shook hands with me. Len was a quiet fellow, an Air Force pilot who had been an instructor at a Texas airfield throughout the war years. Len was over fifteen years younger than myself, but I never felt the difference and called him "Boss Man" all the years of our association together.

That's one of the advantages of military experience you learn to respect the quality of leadership regardless of age or conditions of background.

After our successful interview on that Monday January 5, 1951, Len asked:

"You don't have any children, do you?"
"Yes, Sir, Boss Man. We have two sons."
"Oh, gosh!" exclaimed Len. "Well, don't have any more right away. This job only pays $50.00 a week."

Of course I didn't tell him that Ginny was pregnant with our third son Malcolm, who was born in August of that year. Our fourth, Starr Jr., was born in December of 1952. But I knew I was embarked on the right path. All else would fall into line. And it did, although not without struggle and some surprises.

The work with *Guideposts* proved vastly more intriguing than I had hoped for. Helping people prepare their stories to share with the readers of Guideposts was exciting. These were modern parables. This was religion at work in the marketplace. Some stories that came to us were very well-written, needing only careful editing to fit them into the copy space available for the particular issue in which they would be used. But, most of the stories required considerable work. Some required rewriting to make them intelligible lucid reading. Some people could not write at all, so they had to be interviewed by one of our editors who would prepare the story for them. It requires real editorial skill to interpret people's experiences in words and phrases that reflect the true nature of the person whose experiences are being told.

The skill, and above all the deep spiritual dedication of the *Guideposts* editors, is what has made the magazine such an unusual success in the field of religious journalism. There are many other fine religious magazines but they are essentially the publications of individual churches or particular religious denominations—*The Catholic Digest; The Christian Century; Presbyterian Life* and *The Christian Herald* being among the best. But none of them, except *Guideposts,* is truly interfaith, and interdenominational. I soon learned that many people could not understand how *Guideposts* managed to cross these denominational boundaries when there is so much petty squabbling between various churches. The answer is really very simple.

In telling their individual stories, Guideposts editors explain to the authors that they must not attempt to preach or speak didactically as though interpreting God for everyone. People resent that. However, most people are remarkably tolerant of individual viewpoints, in fact very much interested in the variety of individual human experience, as long as it is presented as uniquely your own, not offered as a pattern for all people to follow. In other words, if you say "this is what happened to me, or this is what I believe the words of Holy Scriptures mean, or this is how I interpret the will of God for my life," readers will accept it and be interested in your story, recognizing that your unique spiritual viewpoint is valid for you, whether they agree with it or not. But, if you say, "This is what God says to the world or this is what Scriptures means for mankind to do..." then the readers resent it, for you are presuming to think for them, and the value of your personal story is lost.

Thus I was delighted to find that the *Guideposts* philosophy coincided with my own, earlier arrived at, viewpoint that man's spiritual hunger finds satisfaction in an amazingly wide variety of religious experience. Actually *Guideposts* was offering its readers a veritable feast of spiritual nourishment. In such an atmosphere of sharing and tolerance, I found hope for a better world and I plunged into the editorial work with relish. Of course, as with any field of endeavor, there were areas where I found my personal views at variance with the organization's policies. But on each of these occasions, overcoming the obstacles to understanding served to broaden my own horizons and, I hope, in some way added to the outlook of the people with whom I worked.

One of my earliest obstacles in the *Guideposts* work was on the form and substance of prayer. The effect of human thought-waves on the growth of plants was much in the current news in the early 50s, as a result of experiments conducted by a former detective. Using the electronic device known as a lie detector, some astonishing results were obtained. One spin-off from these experiments was conducted in California by the Rev. Franklin Loehr, who experimented with prayer, both positive and negative, as a factor controlling plant growth. The spiritual implications intrigued our *Guideposts* editors and we discussed, at out weekly story conference, the possibility that one of us should duplicate the Rev. Loehr's work and tell the results to our readers as a personal experience. Len LeSourd turned to me, "Starr, you're a farmer at heart, and have a keen interest in all growing things. The assignment is yours. Go to it."

Before beginning the actual prayer-seed experiment, I corresponded at length with the Rev. Franklin Loehr, with Dr. J. B. Rhine of the parapsychology laboratory at Duke University, with Dr. Glenn Clark and other persons, here and abroad, who had tried similar work with prayer. Then I began my own experiments which took several weeks and produced two rather startling discoveries. I summarized the results in September of 1954 for *Guideposts*. Herewith are pertinent extracts from my article which I titled:

"Ten Kernels of Corn"

Ten beans, ten cabbage seeds, and ten kernels of corn. I placed them carefully on moist cotton in the tin pan and turned to answer the questioning of my eldest son, aged five and a half.

"No, I'm not planting a garden, Gregory. It's only December. This is just an experiment."

"Can I help?" His eager little fingers were reaching for the yellow grains on the kitchen table.

"I suppose so," I said, not too enthusiastically. Then, watching his eyes light up at the prospect, my reluctance left me. "Yes, sure you can help. Here's a pan for yourself. We'll work together." So I explained to my young son that this was to be an experiment in prayer, which meant talking to God. Gregory was delighted. David (age four) who was watching us, begged to be included in the adventure. So I counted out seeds for him, too.

My basic experiment involved placing two groups of seeds between pieces of moist cotton, and then praying over one group to hasten their germination (sprouting) and add vigor to their growth. But the second seed group is ignored. This latter becomes the control, or check phase, of the experiment.

Gregory and David watched me, now, as I placed identical groups of seeds (usually ten) on each of the moist cotton pads in a muffin tin. Covering these with other pads of moist cotton, I labeled one side "prayer" and the opposite side "control." The boys then prepared their seeds on small pie tins with a string separating the two groups, and we were ready for prayers.

I did not have to explain involved theology or dogmatic forms to my sons. They understood prayer as simple asking, or thanking God for what we need.

When praying I did not use set patterns, but talked sincerely as between close friends, usually something like this:

"Lord, we know that everything in this world exists according to your plan of creation, that this process is still going on at this moment and that you have made us to take part in it, to work with you in producing a better world out of this moment of eternity. Bless these seeds here planted. Make them grow and flourish to the full extent of their being. Do this, we pray, that men may come to understand the power of communication through prayer and faith."

About the third day of the test I told my sons, "We mustn't forget to pray over our seeds again tonight."

"Oh, no. Daddy" replied Gregory, my five year old, "you tell us boys we should ask for things only once and then wait patiently."

I'm sure God must have smiled, as I did, at this boomerang of parental discipline. Needless to say, I did not require them to pray again over their seeds. However, I did pray over mine, on the average of three to four times daily, usually once about midnight before going to bed, and again at 5:00 a.m., before going out to milk (these times looking directly at the seed and placing my hands over them), then, again, while driving to the railroad station, which is my favorite time for morning prayers.

Then at least once again, sometime during my work day in the city, I beamed a prayer request to God over the top of that muffin tin which was setting on a high shelf in our farmhouse kitchen.

Four days later, on Christmas Eve, we checked the experiment and noted these results:

In my pan:	Control	60% germination, with maximum sprouts 2-$^7/_8$" long.
	Prayer	70% germination, with maximum sprouts 2-$^7/_8$" long.

The boys pans: Control 30% germination with maximum sprouts ¹/₉" long.

Prayer 80% germination with maximum sprouts 3" long.

The evidence pointed to positive, measurable gains through prayer, especially that of an unsophisticated child. And succeeding experiments which I have made continue to bear this out.

The Religious Research prayer group used essentially the method described above with similar, though often more dramatic results. The Reverend Loehr tells of one woman in the Research group, "She was devout and accustomed to prayer, but when she joined with the group working on plant growth her seed tests failed. Then she admitted to the others that she had begun the work determined to show how good she was at prayer. Only after she got rid of this pride, and humbly admitted her fault before others, did she begin having success with the prayer plant experiments."

This evidence of the need for soul-searching has been one of the most remarkable results of the work. All persons participating emphasize the necessity to cleanse one's heart and mind before they can direct prayer effectively. And childhood's hearts are already clean. To me this was further proof that "God is not mocked" (Galatians 6:7). He gives us power, tremendous power, through prayer. But it becomes effective only when we use it properly. The measurable evidence of the extent of this power is, I believe, the great value of such experiments as these.

In that light I made one other experiment which deserves inclusion in this report. Following the methods

used by the Rev. Loehr's group, I sprouted two pans of
corn seeds. At the end of six days, sprouts were about
equal, averaging 1-¹/₂" on each pan. Then I began to
pray over both pans. But on the one I prayed for their
continued fruitful growth; on the second (control pan) I
used a negative to stop growth.

After treating both groups with positive and negative
prayer thoughts I did not look at them again. But I continued both prayers, at various times, wherever I might
be.

On checking, two days later, the control group of
seeds receiving negated prayers showed shriveled, almost burned, sprout tips and all growth had stopped. In
the positive prayer group four of the ten seeds had shot
out green stalks over three inches long. The other six
kernels showed continued growth, in lesser degree.

To me this phase of the experiment has the greatest
value of all, for it gives tangible proof of what clergymen, psychologists and psychiatrists have been telling
us for years: that we damage our own lives by our
negative thoughts. The degree of damage reflects the
extent to which we allow destructive ideas to take full
possession of our mind, for mind and soul are one.
Emerson put it so well when he said, "Beware of what
you want to be, for you will become that person."

It's the same secret Jesus pointed out in His parable
of the mustard seed. You can move mountains to you—
or you can pull them down over you! God has made
this power available to every human being whether he
believes in God or not. But, through our religion, we
strive to understand how God wants us to use it for the
betterment of others.

I did not demonstrate the negative prayer phase to my young sons. As they grow older, better able to understand, I will certainly go into it with them, for it is a dramatic lesson and their reactions are enlightening. After all, they are seeds, too, the most precious objects of our continual prayer.

There, then, was the meat of the article. I had enjoyed this story assignment, and the discoveries about prayer success enlarged my own horizons on the subject. As with so many people, my prayers, asking for things I wanted or felt I needed, frequently had gone unanswered. Now, in the third quarter of my life, I had accidentally stumbled on a logical answer:

Man's mind emits thoughts, which have demonstrable energy properties—they can, as Dr. Rhine's experiments had demonstrated,* react upon the material elements of this world. Therefore, thought waves were a form of energy, not unlike electricity. The mind was a transmitting device. If the mind were clouded, fogged with uncertainty or other disturbing influences, its transmission would be blurred, distorted, or otherwise interfered with. Prayer was simply a transmission of the mind, and when the mind (or the heart, its emotional doppler-correction-device) is distorted by hatred, doubt, mistrust or unforgiveness, the transmission is spoiled and the prayer consequently does not reach out to work its effect on the elements of the universe. To me this explained why so many prayers are never answered.

*Reach of the Mind by J. B. Rhine, published 1947 by William Sloane Associates Inc. NYC

Surprisingly, to me at least, this intriguing discovery about negative thought and negative prayer sparked a heated controversy among members of *Guideposts'* editorial board and, as a consequence, "Ten Kernels of Corn" was never printed in the magazine. The deciding vote against its use came from Grace Oursler, (wife of writer and *Reader's Digest* Editor, Fulton Oursler) who felt that dealing with "negative prayer" was akin to talking with the devil. "Grace," I said, "if the devil you believe in truly exists then he must be faced down, not shied away from. He should be discussed, and his power addressed. But if the devil, as I believe, does not really exist at all, then using the evil one as an alibi for not doing something is dodging personal responsibility for facing issues. Come on, let's analyze the subject. This is too important a viewpoint on prayer to be knocked down because of superstition."

Perhaps I shouldn't have used that word superstition, because dear Grace was a sincere and deeply religious woman, and I could see my remarks angered her, for which I was sorry. I only wanted to debate the matter in an objective and, I thought, intellectual manner. But Len LeSourd would not allow it because he feared she might become too emotionally stirred up, and her health was precariously unstable. Reluctantly I let it drop, for I respected Boss Man's judgment. That was one of Len's real talents—he could get people of widely differing viewpoints to work harmoniously together by keeping the larger goal before them. It is a rare talent, possessed by some persons who appear quiet and devoid of the more charismatic qualities which make other leaders stand out, vividly, above their peers. General Dwight Eisenhower was one such leader. Though "Ike" did not have the dramatic personality of such generals as Patton, DeGaule, Montgomery or Spaatzt, yet he could get these "prima donna" types to work smoothly together as a team. Such was the true greatness of Dwight Eisenhower, and my boss man, Len, was of the same mold.

At about this time there was considerable attention, in religious circles, to the theme of being "born again," a spiritual philosophy with which I, myself, was much at odds. I recall that one day a divinity student, assisting at one of our Pawling churches, had called at our house.

I was in the New York office of course, but Ginny was at home, immersed in the hundred and one tasks of raising our four small sons. The young man, enthusiastically extolling the need to be "born again," was trying to convince Ginny that only through participation in such a religious program could anyone hope to truly come into the presence of God.

> "So, until you're born again," said this young evangelist, "you've never really met God."
> "Oh, but I have," replied my wife, "several times."
> "I don't understand," said he.
> Ginny smiled at the seminarian's puzzlement. "Have you ever been present at the birth of a baby?" my wife asked. "Well, I have been through it four times already and each of those moments I stood in God's presence. Did you not know that He is there in that supreme instant of His perfection?"

I would have given a good deal to have watched my Ginny's face as she said it, her brown eyes twinkling with delight, her deep-dimpled smile accenting her pride in those babies and with probably a toss of her tawny red curls challenging the divinity student to top that.

"And what was his answer to that?" I asked Ginny that evening as she recounted the visit.

Ginny laughed. "He didn't say anything. I think I had the young man completely confused. He left immediately afterward."

Another example, I thought, of the failure of religion to reconcile the two sides of the coin, the spiritual and the physical. Especially do I find this evident in the Christian doctrine of the virgin birth. This philosophy, to me, casts discredit upon the manner in which God has created life upon this planet. The idea of a virgin birth demeans conception—the wonderful combining of genes in the creation of a new life, which is the law of nature, and all nature is the work of God.

Granted that mankind has often misused his power of creating by conception, and often debased this vital phase in the chain of Divine evolution. But that does not detract from the sacredness, nor the wonder of the means by which God has ordained man to share in that eternal expansion of the universe.

I have a feeling that the dogma of the virgin birth was created by early founders of Christianity as a means of easing their sense of guilt for man's abuse of his power of procreation. Unfortunately, the succeeding years of guilt relief have not measurably improved man's understanding of his relationship to the Divine cycle. In this age of scientific advance I think it's time that our religious institutions bring their dogma and ritual up-to-date with this century's thinking.

A commendable move to update religious teaching is evident in the campaign of America's Roman Catholic priests who are working to bring about a change in the Vatican's views on abortion and also on celibacy of the priesthood. To the non-Catholic it seems a shocking leftover from feudal times to observe how a celibate priesthood in the Vatican (men who have absolutely no experience with the pain, the mental trauma and the medical facts of childbirth) should assume they have the right (let alone the wisdom) to tell women what to do with their bodies. The American initiative in this matter is an encouraging sign that this great Christian faith is truly moving up to intelligent, religious modernity. How wonderful it would be if they took the lead in realistically reconciling the spiritual and the physical as inseparable sides of the same coin.

I personally saw evidence of this in a conversation I had with a Vietnamese Roman Catholic priest. I was speaking before a mixed group of clergymen at the Army's chaplain school at Fort Hamilton in New York. I was encouraging them to be on the lookout for possible *Guideposts*-type stories among the people they met in the military's far-flung outposts around the world.

In the general discussion, after the sessions, this Vietnamese gentleman spoke up:

> "Being born in what was then called Indochina, I was brought up in the traditions of the religions of the Orient—revering the teachings of Confucius and the Buddha. Then, as an adult, I became a Roman Catholic priest. But I could not thrust from my my mind all the beauty and deep truths embodied in the faith of my people of the Orient. Along with other convert priests of my country we kept bringing these matters to the attention of the Catholic hierarchy in Rome.

And at last we have succeeded in gaining a degree of under-standing. The Holy Father has finally agreed with us that "an-cestor worship," as the western world calls the Oriental prac-tice of revering our progenitors, is in reality nothing less than keeping the "Fourth Commandment"—honoring our fathers and mothers."

This experience of the Vietnamese Catholic priest not only demonstrated real progress in interfaith under-standing, but it acknowledged the reality that physical practice is evidence of the inseparability of the physical and the spiritual in daily life. I reported it to our edi-tors.

At *Guideposts* our weekly editorial staff meetings would often touch on the subject. Some editors saw a very distinct difference between man's physical being and his spiritual self, contending that they could be treated as separate entities, each capable of existence without the other. Some editors, including myself, saw the physical as inseparable from the spiritual—two sides of the same coin. Paradoxically, the broad variety of people's stories coming to *Guideposts* supported both sides of the argument. And all editors agreed on the need to present our readers with stories from the wid-est possible field of human experience.

By now our paid subscriber list had grown to over 1.5 million. Hundreds went to addresses in other coun-tries around the globe, and thousands of more copies were sent, free, to hospitals, nursing homes and U.S. military bases. Thus, each month *Guideposts* printed close to two million copies. Statistics compiled for all commercial magazines showed that an average of four and a half people read each copy of a publication.

Hence a magazine's readership was estimated to be nearly five times the number of magazines printed for each issue. Such figures convinced our editors that we were meeting a very real need for millions of people.

Since we had only an American edition at the time, the religious backgrounds of our *Guideposts* authors were essentially Judeo-Christian, or even agnostic, which is to say they were doubters. Actually many author's stories did not identify the particular creed or denominational division thereof to which they subscribed. We knew it, of course, from correspondence, but, unless the facts were part and parcel of the experience they were relating, it was not lugged into their *Guideposts* article. But, what each story did contain was the factual experience from their personal lives, the spiritual values involved in the events and the reaching out to make contact with the source of creation—the longing to relate to God—the universal need to satisfy spiritual hunger. For this reason *Guideposts* was being received in homes everywhere by people of all religious persuasions.

Frequently at our editorial meetings I had been suggesting that we should publish language editions in other parts of the world, as did the *Reader's Digest.* Then, one day in the summer of 1961, Len told me the magazine's board of trustees had decided to experiment with "foreign editions." Because of my interest in the subject I was assigned the job of developing the project.

At that time I was production editor responsible for "putting the issue to bed," which meant seeing that the manuscripts and art work went to the printers on time, and that each of the several sets of proofs were properly corrected, collated and returned to the printer for the actual press run. This frequently required late work, especially on the days when proofs had to be returned. The other editors would bring their proof corrections to me at the end of the day. I would transfer their mark-ups to the master proof and see that it got back to the printer before midnight. On such nights I would catch the 1 a.m. train to Brewster, be home by 3 a.m., and down to the barn to milk our family cow in the late watches of the night.

This several-times-a-month schedule produced a magical hour which I found most congenial for conversation with my Creator. All the world was quiet; my dear ones were secure and asleep in the farmhouse. Seated, squatting, beside the heifer, I would put my head against her flank and as my fingers rhythmically squeezed the milk into the pail between my knees, I would talk with God. In summer time I would be looking at the night sky through the open barn door, and in winter, perhaps, be watching eddying snow crystals as they slipped through the door crack, settling in tiny white mounds on the concrete floor behind the cow stall. This particular fall night I had important matters to take up with my Creator.

"Well, Lord, here we are again. You, looking down on this complex wonder You have created. And me, facing a fresh challenge to add something new to that complicated, forever evolving, phenomenon here on planet earth."
"So you still find it exciting my son?"
"Oh, definitely. However, You already know that."
"True, but I cannot take man for granted. Since I've given

man free will, I never presume to pre-guess what he will think. So I find it effective, at times, to spur him to re-evaluate by putting his random thoughts into visible structure with words. Thereby he proceeds to visualize—and, what man can conceive within his mind, he can bring forth as accomplished fact. Words, my son, are the building blocks of ideas."

"You mean, Lord, it's up to each of us to develop ideas into patterns, and then build them into reality?"

"Doesn't that answer your demand for purpose in life?"

"Very definitely. So this new idea of *Guideposts* foreign editions could be..."

"Whatever you may visualize with your mind, my son, and shape with your efforts."

"Fine! Then to begin with I won't call them "Foreign Editions." That word is wrong—too many people think of foreign as something unfamiliar, strange, irrelevant or alien. I'll call them "International Editions," for that is what You are, God. *Guideposts International Editions* could be the catalyst which worldwide religions have been needing so desperately—a meeting ground where they can share how they apply spiritual values in their daily lives. The American edition has proved the usefulness of such a publication here in the United States, so I'm going to make it work overseas. Please, Lord, inspire my efforts."

In the next year I corresponded with people around the world, seeking indigenous personnel to undertake the launching of *Guideposts* in their country. To become the publisher-editor of an overseas edition of *Guideposts* we sought individuals who were experienced in publishing or editing and dedicated to the spiritual need of their community; individuals in harmony with *Guideposts* interfaith editorial policy and possessed of an ability to work with people of all religious persuasions; individuals respected in their community for moral integrity, and hopefully, possessed of business acumen. It was quite an order to fill, but find such individuals I did.

In the fall of 1963, we launched our first International Edition, *The Chinese Guideposts,* published in Taipei, Taiwan, Republic of China. Our publisher was the Honorable Elim I.L. Yen, a Certified Public Accountant and member of the Chinese Congress in the democratic government set up by Dr. Sun Yat Sen. Mr. Yen's eldest son, Gordon (a university graduate who spoke English as fluently as his native Mandarin), became our Chinese editor.

Each quarterly issue consisted of a special selection of stories from current and past issues of the American edition. Articles were chosen for their widest appeal. Stories about, and by, people of the Orient were sought and introduced into the issues as they became available. The edition was bilingual, each story being set in parallel columns of Chinese and English. I had decided on the bilingual form as a result of a conference I had with Eleanor Roosevelt at the first meeting of the United Nations in London in 1946.

"English," said Mrs. Roosevelt, "has become the universal language of international government and commerce. It is spoken and understood around the world. No authority ordained it so—it just happened."

The decision to make *Guideposts International Editions* bilingual (we followed the same policy with succeeding editions) proved immensely popular from the very beginning. Within months after our first Chinese edition hit the stands, a radio language-teaching program had been launched in Taiwan, using the Chinese edition as its sole textbook. Soon that radio program was broadcasting half-hour segments, four times a day, six days a week, over Taiwan's three networks. This unexpected spinoff from the *Chinese Guideposts* increased our overseas reader-listenership more than a hundredfold, and became a powerful influence for peace and understanding. For here were thousands of people, striving to learn English, and their textbooks were stories of people resolving life's daily problems by the application of spiritual principles.

In 1964, with our *Chinese Guideposts* completing its first successful year, and a Thai quarterly edition launched in Bangkok, I flew to the Far East to search out other possible editions for the Orient. Traveling through seven countries, from Japan to Indonesia, I found that Orientals had much the same spiritual hunger as *Guideposts* had discovered among Americans.

Especially was this evident in Japan where, in an effort to fill the spiritual vacuum left by demythologizing of the God Emperor, the Japanese people were returning to the Buddhist faith in many revised and new forms. These ranged all the way from the very militant Soge-ga-kai to the very peaceful Rissho-Kosei-Kai*. In this latter faith, established by Nikkya Niwanno,† I discovered people practicing their faith in a religious service that very much resembled a meeting in America of the "Layman's Movement for a Christian World." Here, indeed, I thought is an area where readers of our international *Guideposts* will be able to share experi-

*Rissho Kosei-Kai Pub. by Kosei, Tokyo 1966.
†Templeton Award winner 1979, for "Progress in Religion"

ences that will enrich believers of all faiths. And I set out to bring about a Japanese edition. But the Japanese, for all that in the past they had copied much of what the Western world created, are a most independent minded people. I would seem very close to getting a Japanese *Guideposts* launched, and then it would evaporate.

Years later, on another trip to Japan I visited Mr. Knosuke Matsushita the president of Panasonic Industries, who was also the founder of an inspirational magazine called PHP*. I had hoped for a personal story from Matsushita that we could carry in *Guideposts International Editions*. But this quiet, self-effacing Japanese gentlemen kept insisting that he was not a religious man, though it seemed to me that everything he did in life was for the good of others. Here, I thought is a living example of the parable about the good Samaritan. But Matsushita would not allow me to prepare a story about him that would show him as being in any way religious. Though disappointed, I admired his sincerity and had to respect his wishes.

In the course of our talk I discovered that, right after World War II, Matsushita in Japan, like Pinky Thornburg in America, had decided that Japanese businessmen should become the leaders in a new approach to moral integrity for his nation. Matsushita told me that he had called together the heads of Japanese industry and said it was up to them to bring Japan back into good repute in the family of nations. In the

---

*PHP is a monthly periodical. "Published as a forum... from which the problems we face in life, and society, may be seriously discussed by people of various races religions, cultures, ages, and organizations around the world."

past, he told them, Japan was noted, worldwide, for making cheap copies of Western goods. Now disgraced by a brutal war which they had inflicted upon the world, their only hope to regain world respect would be to take the lead in creating a new climate for honesty and integrity in world trade. Matsushita said to his countrymen:

> "Japan must stop making shoddy copies of Western goods. We must turn out only the best possible products of which we are capable. We have the talent. What we need now is the determination to produce only the finest. I have already instructed the management of all Matsushita electrical plants that they are to turn out only superior products made with the very best materials. If we make a profit, well and good. But profit will be secondary to manufacturing the very highest quality product we can achieve. Nothing else will do. I challenge the businessmen of Japan to join me in this new economic venture."

The results of that dynamic leadership* are now a matter of history. Japan has become a world leader in industry and, I observe, the individual Japanese worker is a happy and satisfied laborer because he recognizes that he is responsible for helping to create a better world for those who will follow. This feeling provides real satisfaction to man's spiritual hunger. It gives purpose to his life. It is something which the American working man needs desperately and seems unable to

---

*The Matsushita Phenomenon" by Rowland Gould: Diamond Publishing Co. Tokyo

find on his job today. I believe it is because he has lost pride in the product of his brain and brawn. The American worker has learned that too much of what he produces is an inferior product. The standards of today's manufacture are not quality, but quantity and low cost. Unfortunately, our labor unions, by limiting how much effort they will permit a worker to put into a job, have done much to kill the work ethic. Thus many an American worker, seeing only wages and fringe benefits as the reward for his efforts, remains spiritually hungry and physically dissatisfied with his job.

But to go back. That 1964 trip to the Orient did produce results for *Guideposts*. Though Tokyo excited me with its possibilities and disappointed me with its realities, on the other side of the Japan Sea I found a totally different response. In South Korea I met Ho NamKung, son of Korean shipping magnate Ryuan NamKung. Young Ho had visions for his nation beyond economic independence. He wanted to help his people acquire broad horizons in the matter of ethics and moral values, for therein he felt lay the path to useful world leadership. I carried Ho NamKung's dream back to our magazine's executive board.

In January of 1965 the *Korean Guideposts* became our third overseas edition. With the farsighted Ho Nam-Kung as its publisher, the Korean edition soon advanced from quarterly to monthly issues and, following the pattern set by our Chinese edition, also established a radio program for learning English. Using the Magazine as its textbook, the *Korean Voice of Guideposts* broadcasts daily over three networks that reach all of

North and South Korea as well as islands in the Japan sea.

Within the next four years I was able to create three more international editions:

A *Swedish Guideposts,* published by Haakon Cronlsioe in Stockholm; a *British Guideposts,* published by Raymond Cripps in England's Oxfordshire village of Witney, and a *Latin American Guideposts,* a bilingual Spanish-English edition, published by Manuel Flores and Lopes Delara in Mexico City. They were indigenous personnel of their respective countries, wonderful people to work with, all deeply spiritual and in harmony with *Guideposts'* interfaith policy. My own faith was deepened and expanded by association with them and the many people of other nations whom I met in the course of this exciting phase of my life.

One of my most important spiritual discoveries came as a result of a conversation I had with a man from Bombay. This gentleman from India, now a Lutheran minister, had come to my office in New York City. We were discussing my hopes of a *Guideposts* edition for India. Knowing how deeply religious are the people of India, I was telling him I thought it would be great to have these people sharing their experiences with the readers of our international *Guideposts* editions.

"But they are not Christian," said my friend from India.

"Of course not," I replied, "but they are human beings, they are God's creatures, the same as you and I. They have spiritual hunger that reaches out to touch the Source of Creation. The course of their daily lives is affected by the values they believe in."

"But isn't *Guideposts* a Christian magazine?"

"Not exclusively. Of course, the stories in the American edition are primarily from people who are of the Jewish or Christian faiths, because those are the principal religious persuasions of this country. But in our international editions, we will be seeking out stories from people of all religions in the countries where they publish. We cannot be honestly interfaith (as our masthead statement proclaims us to be) unless our pages are open to sharing the experiences of all devout people. Remember, *Guideposts* articles do not discuss the dogma, ritual or theological premises of any of the many different religious faiths, for these are the manmade areas which divide us. But, what unites us is the existence of the Divine Source of Creation. And *Guideposts* stories are simply the true experience of people reaching out to God (by whatever name he is called) in an effort to apply universal spiritual truths to meeting the problems of living on this planet in this moment of eternity.

"The particular piece of the pie of religious truths, that each person finds satisfies his or her individual spiritual hunger, should not become a division between us, for all faiths nourish the soul. The philosophers of India have described this very logical spiritual law as like unto a giant wheel, with many spokes radiating out from the hub to the rim. The various religions are the spokes—their differences being greater at the rim and diminishing the closer they get to the hub—which is God. If *Guideposts* were exclusively a Christian magazine it would not be really Christian at all, for it would be locking out our brothers, thus contradicting a basic premise of Christianity. Isn't that so?"

"But what about Jesus?" replied the Lutheran minister from Bombay. "Jesus said, 'I am the way, the truth and the light. None entereth unto the Father except by me!' That's what the Bible says, plain and to the point. How do you get around that Mr. Jones?"

"You don't get around it, you dig into it," I replied. "Listen my friend, all my life that particular statement, attributed to Jesus by the Gospel of John (written almost a hundred years after the death of the Carpenter), has disturbed me. It is so illogical, so didactic, so unlike the nature of the humble Man of Nazareth. I tell you that over the years I have many times argued this point with God. So, now, I'll try to put into words for you the answers that evolved.

"First I made a study of the teachings of Jesus—the writings by Matthew, Mark and Luke, on what Jesus said and what he did. And I discovered it could all be summed up in one word— love. I further noted that Jesus was a truly humble man, never one to push himself, seldom one to use the personal pronouns I, me or mine. Mostly in matters of spiritual authority he referred to God the Father. So secondly, I took that irritating phrase from St. John and for every personal pronoun used in that statement I substituted the word which is the essence of Jesus' teaching—love. And this is how I found it to read: "Love is the way, the truth and the light, none entereth unto the Father except by love." So, there you have it. Through prolonged debate with God I had finally arrived at a totally new concept, one that was logical, one that fits the nature of Jesus as the gospels of Matthew, Mark and Luke had revealed Him to us."

I looked at the face of my friend from Bombay. His eyes were smiling happily, and for an instant I knew I was once more looking on the countenance of the Creator.

"Thank you for that explanation," said he. "You have relieved my heart, greatly. You see I was raised in the Hindu faith. Then as a young man, I converted to Christianity. But my mother and father have remained devout Hindus to this day. And it has troubled me that my Christian faith has cut me off from them. But the way you've just explained it sheds an entirely different light on the words of Jesus—and in that context I see we can never be separated, regardless of the path by which we reach out to God. Thank you again, my friend."

It was a rewarding moment for me, too, for in sharing with this good man from India the sum of my discourse with God, I knew I had uncovered an abiding truth. In the years since then I have found it applicable to many of the other contradictory statements made in the Gospel of John. I truly believe both John and his translators, in an attempt to create a rigid theology out of the teachings of the gentle Nazarene, had done Jesus an injustice that shut him off from a large sector of God's creatures to whom, in his short life, he had been reaching out with an all-encompassing love.

At other times, during my long and involved editorship with *Guideposts,* there were moments of revelation about the nature of man and his hunger for contact with God that were often humorous and sometimes disturbing. I recall that while developing our overseas editions I frequently visited people at the Carnegie Building for International Peace on East 46th Street overlooking the United Nations. One day, while attending a reception there, I was chatting with my friend Dr. Daniel Lew, permanent representative to the United Nations from the Republic of China. Daniel was also very active in the work of moral re-armament. I had keen admiration for the dedicated people of this movement because they believed they could change this world for the better by first changing themselves—and they recognized God by whatever name people chose to call him. As we talked, Daniel noticed a new arrival, whom he said was one of the most influential executives in our State Department.

"But of course you know him," said Daniel.
"No," I replied, "I've never met him."
"Well. I know him quite well," said Daniel. "Come with me," whereupon he steered me over to the group that was

greeting the new arrival. Daniel introduced me, concluding with, "You two should have much in common."

The man from the State Department looked me over with ill concealed lack of interest.

"And just what do you and I have that has something in common?" he asked as we shook hands perfunctorily.
"God," I replied. "God and His purpose for this world."
The State Department official almost choked on his drink. "Yes, yes, of course," he replied and quickly moved to the other side of the room.

How sad, I thought. For it appears to me that this same lack of concern for the larger moral aspect of world affairs seems to infect so many of the people working at the United Nations. And they are not only people of our own country but also personnel from the other countries meeting in those solid, concrete buildings erected beside the East River. I often wonder if any of them ever pause to reflect on the rigidity of those beautiful, manmade structures compared with the yielding, majestic God-created waters that flow silently beside their very foundations. Are they aware that this same parallel evidence of the two sides of the coin of life exists, coincidentally, in many of their nation's seats of government? The United States Capitol on the Potamac; Britain's magnificent buildings of Parliament beside the Thames; Canada's beside the Ottawa River, even Egypt's beside the Nile. One wonders, sometimes, how some men, in carrying out God's purpose on this planet can be so absorbed in the work of their own hands that they are oblivious to the source from which their power derives.

I once had a discussion with Dr. Peale on the matter of man's preoccupation with his own creativity. We were talking about Norman's frequent articles in *Guideposts* on the subject of fear.

"I talk about it often," said Norman, "because I find most people are full of fear. They write me letters about their fear. They come to me after church services or after my frequent lectures around the country—they want to discuss their fears."

"Many people perhaps, Norman, but I would not say most people," I replied. "I believe those people filled with fear are essentially those who live in cities where they are almost completely surrounded by the work of their own hands and minds—the buildings they live in, the vehicles they move in, the foods they have manufactured and the clothes they wear— man has made them all—and they have fallen short of providing the total satisfaction he seeks—hence fears easily assail them."

"But you will not find those same fears, Norman, consuming those of us who live in the country or close to the land. For we are daily surrounded by the evidence of God's creativity—we see in nature the wonder and perfection of life as God has produced it on this planet. So, with this broad horizon of perspective we are able to see our own creativity, both in its limitations and its place in advancing the evolution of God's law as it is being carried out by nature. Thus we have assurance of our purpose in the scheme of things, and we have no fears, such as seem to plague the complete city dweller."

Later on, as we worked together, I saw a surprising example of Norman's sharp perception in spiritual matters. But what surprised me even more was the reluctance of some *Guideposts* editors to tell our readership about it. It came about in this manner We were preparing a brief report on an extended trip of Norman's around the world. We had several news clips from overseas papers from which we gleaned small anecdotes we thought might be of interest to *Guideposts'* readers. One news story, from Karachi, Pakistan, carried a most intriguing item:

The Rotary Club of Karachi had given a luncheon in Dr. Peale's honor. After the luncheon these Pakistani Rotarians gathered around Dr. Peale, plying him with questions. In order to allow clearing of the dining room, the crowd of questioners and Dr. Peale were moved to another room. There, for an hour or more, these Pakistani gentlemen carried on an intense, informal discussion with Dr. Peale on religious matters. At the conclusion of the period Dr. Peale told them that it had been one of the most inspiring, spiritual experiences of his life. Then, on an impulse, he asked how many in the crowded room were Christians. Only two raised their hands. Dr. Peale was amazed. Here he had spent over an hour in a most stimulating spiritual discourse with a room full of men who were devout Moslems. Commenting about it afterward, Dr. Peale said that maybe we can learn much from our bretheren whose path to God is other than our own.

I thought this was a wonderful example of insightful growth on the part of Dr. Peale. Certainly it should be included in our *Guideposts* report. But, to my astonishment, the other editors did not agree at all. Said one editor (a most erudite journalist), "We cannot tell our readers that after a lifetime of Christian ministry, Dr. Peale has suddenly discovered elements of truth in another religion. No. We just cannot do that."

I was completely flabbergasted at such narrowness of viewpoint. But, though I argued hard to include what

I felt was a beautiful story of mental and spiritual progress, the anecdote was not included in the *Guideposts* story of Dr. Peale's trip—the American edition that is. But I did carry the complete story in all of my international editions and received many favorable comments on the breadth of Dr. Peale's understanding.

I mention the story here because it is an example of "opinion journalism," the character fault which afflicts much of our media today. Fortunately, it had seldom touched *Guideposts* before, because we insist that our authors speak for themselves.

When I found that contemporary writers, even those whose integrity I respected, would intentionally allow, by omission or otherwise, actual events to be thus misreported it disturbed me greatly. I don't know if Norman ever knew about it, or what he would have felt about it. But he was not the only man to have been incorrectly recorded by his contemporaries—for even the Disciples (with best of intentions so it would seem) misrepresented the Carpenter.

Misrepresentation, or misunderstanding, must surely be accounted as one of the chief reasons why man has so often failed to learn from the errors of those who have gone before him. Especially do I find this true in the area of moral values and human character development. Maybe for the very reason that they are intangible, abstract and difficult to nail down, the evidence of their reality is observable only in looking backward at the behavior of man himself. Yet their importance to human progress is perhaps more critical than all the very tangible scientific advances man has made. For those advances are carrying us forward, today, with such terrific momentum that, unless man's character development can begin to match his scientific progress, and control it, we may very well scorch our planet—this beautiful globe the evolution of which God has entrusted to us.

But, to use a modern metaphor, the fire insurance we seek will not be found in throwing away our scientific instruments. In the application of man's divinely implanted urge to meet the challenge of existence, we have unlocked some of the secrets of the universe. Now we must learn to live with, and use, that knowledge for the further evolution of mankind. Nuclear energy is, today, a fact of 20th century scientific reality. We can't run from it, ignore it, or lock it back into the eternal unknown from which it was uncovered. A superior man must rise to manage and control it, not hide in fear of it.

Then how do we go about bringing man's character development abreast of his technological advances? How do we train him to master the creations of his brain? It seems to me we have to begin with the way we bring up our children: the hope we instill in them, the moral values we pass on to them, the spiritual strength we cultivate in their eager, receptive minds, in the years from infancy until they depart for college. And the most powerful tool for that instruction of a child is the personal example we set as parents.

This certainty I have arrived at from years of personal experience. My wife and I raised our four sons to manhood during the difficult years of the dawning atomic age. We battled at first hand the inadequacies of public school education in matters of discipline, low standards for quality of work submitted, and re–moval of "incentive-through-competition" in scholastic achievement. To counteract these deficiencies we encouraged their young minds to expand as they met the challenge offered in Cub and Boy Scout programs; they gained self confidence through raising and exhibiting their animals in the 4H Club shows at the County Fair.

Then, in the dark days of the sixties and seventies, while many of their schoolmates took to drugs, and desertion to escape from military responsibilities, we were proud to support the free choice of our sons as they joined high school and college ROTC units, later volunteered for active military service in Vietnam, then followed that with continuing service in Reserve and National Guard units. During all of this I, myself, continued in weekly Army Reserve and summer encampment training as infantry commandant with the New York USAR School.

We participated in our sons' education by joining PTA activities, attending school open-house nights and fighting fiercely when bureaucratic teachers and school administrators sought to perpetuate mediocrity in education with curricula that eliminated competition from classroom studies.

We became Cubmaster and Den Mother and Scout troop committee members. We taught adult leadership classes. We recruited and cajoled other parents to serve with us in these volunteer youth leadership positions. But we were continually appalled at the apathy of some mothers and fathers, who, having brought their children into the world, simply allowed them to shift for themselves as they struggled into adulthood.

Many parents were glad to have their children in Scout or 4H programs for the training advantages they offered, but others were interested only in the hours of childcare which the programs provided. And, sadly, far too many parents simply refused to give any of their personal time to helping with these activities.

Unfortunately, such parents seemed not to realize that by their selfish behavior they were cheating their children at a most vital stage of their growing up. These are the critical years when values are being formed into character traits which will become either bulwarks, or obstacles, in their adult life. These are the times when children, observing adult behavior, make value judgments based on the discrepancies between what is taught in the home, school or church (about morality and religion) and what their parents actually do in their everyday lives. This is the area where misrepresentation begins to color their viewpoint of life. After a child reaches 18, no college class, no military training course, no business or marriage experience, can untwist the moral fibers already woven into a youth's character, nor redo the behavior patterns which form the structure of their unique personalities.

These were the concerns which occupied our minds as Ginny and I launched into the task of raising our sons—our "quadsquad" as I called them, for they arrived in cadence, from 1948 to 1952. At that time our own church, the non-denominational Christ Church on Quaker Hill (where they were all baptized) was only a part-time parish ministering to the summer residents of the area. So, for year round continuity of Sunday School instruction, we sent them to the local Pawling

Methodist Church. This proved fortunate because the pastor there had great rapport with youth and the Church School was a thriving activity. Here the boys received a good grounding in basic theology and in Scriptures—the record of man's spiritual seeking.

Friends, who knew our personal preference for a very broad religious faith, were surprised that we chose a particular denominational church in which to have our sons learn about spiritual values. We told them the denominational division was not important, that was only a man-created spiritual boundary, but what was important was God the Creator, and He would be found in any church. Something of this we explained to our sons, telling them that as they grew older we expected them to choose their own church affiliations depending on where each boy found spiritual nourishment. What was all-important, we told them, was getting to know God. The different religions and denominations were simply different paths leading us to the Creator.

Prayers, in our home, were mostly at mealtime. At the table we would talk, informally, with God, expressing appreciation for life and blessings. Since without food we could not exist, it seemed the most natural time to communicate with our Creator who provided it, and also to recognize the hands that prepared it. Besides saying grace before meals, I had taught the boys to raise their glasses (with water, milk or whatever they had to drink) and offer a toast to their mother as a gesture of thanks. Sometimes we said, "Your health, Mother" or simply ".To the ladies!"

Our dining table at the farm was set against a long window that faced a magnificent view across the valley. The four boys sat on one side, facing the window. Ginny and I sat at each end. One day, as we began our lunch our number three son, Malcom, then about seven years old, raised his glass of milk toward the window and the sky beyond as he proclaimed in a happy voice: "Your health, God!" Needless to say the rest of us joined in the toast. I mention this not because it is a cute story but because it demonstrates the naturalness with which children learn to look upon God when they find Him a part of their home life. Our oldest son, Greg, once, when he was about nine or ten, was standing with his brothers under the drooping branch of a golden weeping willow tree near the barn. It was early spring. The willow buds were just bursting forth in feathery green-gold and I was explaining to the boys about the cycle of nature, when young Greg threw up his arms and exclaimed, "Oh, I love God!"

Certainly, Ginny and I love Him for having given us four fine sons to raise. I tried to tell God this one night in the midst of a wild summer storm. The lightning and thunder were so fierce that Ginny and I had scrambled from our bed to check on the children. But all four were sound asleep—two babies in one crib and two small lads in the other. As we stood there in our night robes, our arms around each other, our heads bent over the little ones, the lightning became a continuous white flare on the walls and the thunder one long crashing roll. But we felt no fear, only gratefulness.

"Thank you, Lord," I said half aloud. "These boys you've entrusted to our care are surely as wonderful a treasure as all the crops which will grow up from this rainfall. We'll strive to raise them in such manner that their individual personalities, and the efforts of their lives, will be a force to better this world, maybe even as powerful as Your thunder and lightning which are now announcing the blessing of Your rainfall over the earth."

The raising of our sons occupied our every effort for some 25 years, giving us unbounded joy, and a fair share of obstacles. In order that the reader may better appreciate what I want to tell you in this chapter about those boys, a thumbnail picture of each is appropriate at this point. Now, while my Ginny has lovely red hair, that burst of flame did not appear in our offspring until our sons began presenting us with grandchildren. All four of our sons have dark hair and eyes, and good figures that eventually topped out around the six-foot mark. But their individual natures are as different as liberal left is from conservative right.

Greg, our oldest son, was a highly imaginative lad, hiding a sensitive nature under a bold reaching-out to embrace the challenges of life. He was the first to join the 4-H, exhibiting his hamshire ewes with which he won many prize ribbons at our Dutchess County Fair. He was our first Eagle Scout, later our first ROTC Cadet. Several times a week he would leave for high school at 6:30 a.m. in order to spend a voluntary hour, before classes, practicing with the exhibition rifle drill team. The more difficult the challenge, the more readily Greg would strive to conquer it. After college he volunteered for active duty with the Army's Armored Corps, then he took flight training and earned his wings as a helicopter pilot, in which capacity he served in Vietnam. Shot down three times behind enemy lines, Greg always managed to get back to resume the fighting. He told us he developed great respect for the South Vietnamese people and their desire to remain free of totalitarian rule. Especially did he admire the courage of the Montagnard soldiers.

In the matter of religion Greg was a pragmatist and something of an agnostic. Yet, while still in high school he was attracted to the ritual and thinking of the Roman Catholic faith, in which he took lengthy instruction. Since we had always encouraged each boy to choose for himself the church where he found the greatest spiritual nourishment, Greg eventually became a Catholic.

David, our second son, was the most serious of the boys. While he and Greg were continually at odds (in the traditional sibling rivalry between oldest and second child) David looked up to Greg and followed his lead in most activities. He also joined the 4-H program, as did his younger brothers, Malcolm and Starr. But David and Malcolm raised Angus and Hereford beef steers, while Starr Junior raised sheep, the same as Greg. All three followed their oldest brother through scouting and on into the high school and college ROTC Cadet ranks. But, in matters religious, David was our most deeply devout son. For several years he worshipped in the Episcopal Church (which he attended with his aunt, my sister, Isobel) and seriously considered entering the ministry of that faith.

Then, in his second college year, David discovered the doctrine of the Mormon Church. One particular tenant of the Latter Day Saints faith states that according to Scriptures, all men are by right members of the priesthood of God. Therefore, no hierarchy of ordained ministers conducts the Mormon church services. But every young man of that faith, when he reaches his twelfth birthday, becomes a member of the Aaronic priesthood and is instructed, among other things, in how to conduct the sacraments of Holy Communion and Baptism. Therefore, at Mormon worship services, these young men of the congregation bless the bread and water of the Holy Eucharist and pass it to their fellow church members. This element of the faith appealed strongly to our David's views on spiritual matters and he joined the church. In the Mormon community David found great and continuing satisfaction.

Malcolm, our third son, was our blithe spirit, with a ready smile and the soul of an artist. His talents in this direction showed up early in school where he was soon drawing and painting as though he had been taught by one of the old masters. But he was impatient of these skills and ignored our encouragement to cultivate them. It was not until his junior year in college that Malcolm decided, on the advice of a stranger, no less, to seriously major in that field, finally graduating with a bachelor's degree in fine arts. But, it was this sensitivity to line and beauty, we believe, that gave Malcolm his feelings of deep compassion and his tolerant appreciation for mankind's wide variety of spiritual beliefs.

While Malcolm eventually followed David into the Mormon Church (though for quite different reasons) we believe our number three son will always be able to find God, whether in or out of an organized church, and in whatever background through which the circumstance of life may lead him.

Also different from his other brothers, our youngest son, Starr, was the most independent of them all. "I do it myself," was one of the first complete phrases he uttered. And he kept on saying it as he grew older. He wanted no help from others—he would do it entirely by himself. I remember so well when he first exhibited his sheep in the 4-H Club arena at the Rhinebeck Fair. He had a large Hampshire ram which he had raised. Little Starr (as we called him then) was only about nine years old at the time. Starr's ram, Sam, was a big handsome animal, looking larger than ever with his fleece curried and groomed so that all the white hairs on his back stood up making a straight, carefully clipped, surface that was beautiful to see. Little Starr—not much taller than the ram itself, stood by his head waiting for the signal to lead the animal into the show ring. The waiting was making the ram restless and I was concerned that he might bolt and spoil the boy's chances for the showmanship prize.

"Maybe you'd better put the halter on him," I cautioned Little Starr. My son gave me a withering glance.

"That spoils the appearance of the head!"

"Then, maybe you'd better let your brother help you. Sam's awfully strong and he weighs close to 200..." I spoke hastily for I saw the ringmaster's signal.

"Dad, I will handle him myself!" Whereupon our youngest son put his right hand under the ram's beautiful black head where he grabbed a handful of fleece, placed his left hand carefully on the big sheep's well-groomed rump and, talking confidently to the restless animal, led Sam into the center of the sawdust ring. No one could have been prouder than little

Starr as he paraded his animal before the judges, no one, except perhaps his mother and father watching from behind the corral bars.

When it came to spiritual matters little Starr kept his own counsel and seemed quite happy with the philosophy he found in the Methodist Church. Later, while in his last year of college, he married a girl of Methodist faith and continued with regular attendance of other parishes during the first years of their married life.

Now, since this book is essentially about my personal search to satisfy spiritual hunger, it has not been my intention to involve the reader in the adult lives of our four sons or their own reaching out to God. But something in Starr Junior's early religious experience was so unusual that I feel I should digress for a moment to include it at this point.

We had encouraged our sons to choose their own colleges. Gregory picked Wentworth Military Academy in Lexington, Missouri, and David selected Utah State University at Logan. Malcolm and Starr Jr. followed Greg to Wentworth for their first years of college and then went on to Utah for their junior and senior years, Malcolm choosing David's Utah State at Logan while Starr chose Weber State at Ogden, Utah, the city where I was stationed briefly in World War II. As I've already told, you David and Malcolm found spiritual nourishment among the Mormon people of Utah and there joined the Church of Latter Day Saints before they finished college. But Starr (we of course stopped calling him "Little Starr" when he left for college and substituted his proper designation, Starr Junior), this fourth son found no affinity with the Mormon Church. Though he and his wife lived many months in the Utah homes of his two brothers while finishing college and later taking post-graduate credits there, both Starr and Jeanne said they were quite definitely not attracted to the Mormon faith.

Then, some three years after college, while stationed with the U.S. Coast Guard on Cape Cod in Massachusetts, Jeanne and Starr surprised us all by joining the Mormon Church. Starr Jr., in a letter to us, explained their decision by saying: "...when we lived in their homes we observed that both David and Malcolm had unusually warm and harmonious relationships with their wives. There was peacefulness in their home life that we wished, earnestly, we could create in our own. We had talked about it often and finally came to the conclusion that the intangible tranquillity within their home was something they derived from their religion. We decided we wanted that for ourselves. We then sought out the local Mormon Church, took several weeks of instruction and joined."

True to his independent nature ever since childhood, even into adult thinking about spiritual matters, our now-grown-big fourth son, had chosen for himself his pathway to communicate with God. And, as had his brothers, Starr found great satisfaction from his personal seeking.

Now to go back. During our son's high school days all three of the younger boys took a very active part in several community productions of the youthful musical *Up With People*. This spiritual and patriotic production was the inspiration of Moral Re-Armament, one of the finest ecumenical religious movements ever to capture the imagination of American youth. We were grateful that our sons had the opportunity to work with these spiritually dedicated people. The boys particularly enjoyed the association with the young men and women who created and performed *Up With People*. It was an unusual experience in cooperation, self-discipline and high moral principles in the production of entertainment, qualities of character building which were sadly lacking in boy's public school classes at that time.

It was when the lack of discipline in our local public school became too damaging to our sons' scholastic progress that we were faced with a difficult decision. There was no parochial school nearby. The cost of private schools was beyond our means, and we disliked the idea of boarding schools, believing that until they go away to college children need the warmth and love, the caring of parents, to come home to after school each day. It was the boys who made the decision.

In addition to wanting a school that could maintain orderly classes, the boys had expressed the desire for ROTC training. While this excellent program of instruction was available at most colleges, Junior ROTC (the high school level program), was offered by only four schools in our New England area. So, after careful reconnaissance, we settled on the high school in New Bedford, Massachusetts, the fishing port city of Moby Dick fame. Securing a house there, we entered all four sons in the public schools of that old whaling town. Being the second most important fishing port in the United States, New Bedford attracted immigrants from all the middle eastern countries—Lebanon, Turkey,

Iran, Iraq and others, as well as immigrants from Greece and Portugal. This multi-national population, many of them first generation Americans, was keenly aware of the advantages offered by American citizenship, and they were proudly patriotic. None of the negativism, which was then infecting so much of our entire East Coast, was to be found in New Bedford. We think the boys gained as much from their association with those enthusiastic Americans as they did from the excellent public school system there.

During the five years we maintained a home in New Bedford, Ginny stayed there with them. But, since I had to carry on my editor's job with *Guideposts,* I remained "batching it" on the farm, commuting by train to New York City each day. Then, on Friday evening, I would take the bus to New Bedford, remaining through Sunday night and returning to work in NYC on Monday morning.

Then, one night on the farm, I had a dream, a dream so vivid that I sat up in bed, wide awake and shaken. For in the dream the Lord had appeared to me and said that my time was up. I was to leave this world the very next day. I protested that our sons were not raised. There was much that I had not yet instructed them about. But the Lord said I would have to put it in a letter to them for I must leave without seeing them again.

I don't know how long I sat there in the dark, combing my mind to extract the essence of what I should have told them. At last I got up and started writing. Dawn came before I had finished so I decided to go to work and complete the task that evening.

During that day I thought of calling New Bedford, but decided against it because my voice breaks easily when I'm emotionally involved and I didn't want to disclose my dream instructions until I had completed the letter. But the thought of talking to them physically absorbed me—so I decided to put the letter on tape. When I got home that night I set up my recording equipment, then sat down and finished the letter in longhand, because I've never been able to write creatively on a typewriter.

I finished the letter about midnight and started to record. But my voice sounded so flat I stopped. Quickly I sorted through my collection of classical music and pulled out several records whose melodies matched my mood. Then, sitting on the fireplace fender of our dining room, with the tape recorder, record player, microphones and sheets of writing spread out on the floor before me, I combined then on the tape and talked out, to our sons, the advice and instructions my dream had commanded me to make. The music, soft in the background, was a help, and I did not follow strictly my written letter.

The birds were starting to welcome the dawn outside as I finished. Of course, much of what I said was too personal to have meaning beyond our family circle. But what I had to say about certain values, spiritual and otherwise, seems pertinent to this work so, with the permission of our sons, I want now to share with you some of what I wrote to them that night:

"Windy farm, May, 1968. Greg, David, Malcolm and Starr. Dearest Sons:
The wonderful years of your growing up are almost com-

pleted. Soon you will each turn off, on a road of you own choosing, toward a career and a family of you own. Your mother and I have worked, and loved dearly, helping you to reach this desired adulthood.

As we look back on those 16 to 20 years of joyous, sometimes tumultuous, but always heartwarming times of our family life, Ginny and I are filled with such sweet and poignant memories that our hearts continually sing together. We hope that your own marriages will be as richly rewarding. Yet Ginny and I find ourselves now approaching the intersection of life's crossroads with not much still to be said or done. But this tape is your father's effort to sum up, for the both of us, what we would want you to remember, and to carry with you as guidelines on your own life's journey..."

Accordingly, on the tape, I proceeded to offer each son some words of recognition for his particular talents, and to counsel continuing efforts toward correcting his individual shortcomings. After that, and a few words on general conduct, I said to them:

"Trust and treat all men with respect. Be ever courteous to women. Be thrifty. Save one third of all money you earn or secure. Pay your way as you go—remembering that it is dishonest to buy comfort or luxury for yourself before paying any obligation you have contracted for services rendered, or goods already consumed..."

Then I told them that among my papers I had come across two letters which I had written, some years earlier, addressed to our sons. I felt they somehow summed up all else I now wished to pass on to them. The first letter I had written on the train to New York,

It was dated the twenty-third of April 1965. So I read it aloud on the tape, and here is part of that recording:

"Dear Beloved Sons:

As I write the date above I realize that today it's just 24 years since I first reported for duty in the United States Army, to begin one of the most important phases of my life.

"I have been proud of the privilege of serving my country. It is a great nation, I pray it does not now go down the slow path of moral disintegration that the republic of the Romans followed. It has taken so many centuries for men to learn the secret of freedom of the individual...

"Sons, these are indeed the times that try men's souls. And they cry out for leaders—men who are not afraid, men who still have vision, to lead American upward again. The world looks to the United States for the kind of leadership which a free soil grows. Remember, Sons, America has the longest consecutively operating form of government on earth today. No other country has been governed so long by the same constitution...

"Yes, Dear Sons, never forget that. And don't let anyone sell you short on your country; there are plenty trying to do it today. But I know that each of you will in your own way when the responsibilities of leadership are pressed on your doorstep, rise to the occasion and accept, boldly, the privilege of serving your fellowman, without ever a thought of what's in it for you...

"I'm not talking just about your military obligation to your country. I know you each feel it, and will serve with honor when your time comes for active duty...But I'm talking especially about your responsibility to make America better—a finer, safer, pleasanter place to live in. Remember the motto we used to have in our Cub Scout pack—Leave it better—well, that's a pretty good guide for life, Sons."

"I wrote that letter four years ago. It seems even more important today. And how heartening it is, to

Ginny and myself, that you boys have made so much progress these four years...

"Well, now let me read you that second letter. I find I wrote it fifteen years ago. It is dated: midnight, March 25, 1954. I said:

"Dearest Sons,

We have just retucked you all in your beds, said a prayer of thanks to God, for sending you to us to brighten our lives, and it occurs to me that you will be wondering, before many more years, about that same God perhaps finding yourselves in doubt about Him.

"As you grow up, dear Sons, and watch man's stupid squabbles about God, in their confusing maze of theologies, dogmas, rituals and allegiances, you may doubt God's very existence, for you will see men praise His teachings in church, synagogue or temple, yet fail to practice those teachings in their daily lives.

"But, do not be disturbed in your hearts concerning these surface muddyings of the river of life. Learn to bear with your fellowman in his stumbling, reaching out toward the light of Divine Power. Know sons, in your heart, that God does exist, even as this wonderful world, which he created, exists. Don't worry about which brand of religion claims the greatest efficacy, or supremacy, in revealing God's truth. Remember, all soaps clean—what is important is the sanitary results of the use of soap—that is more important than the name of the product itself. So, take the 'name brands' of religion tolerantly—humorously if you like, and look beyond their advertised claims to the more important values, the results they achieve in making a better place out of this world which God has entrusted to our care.

"And, don't worry about the next world, take first things first. Concentrate on doing your utmost to understand, and help unfold, the wonders of this visible world where God has placed us, in this moment of eternity. Only in that way will you develop any ability to cope with the other worlds which will follow your life on this one.

"Sons, look for heaven, not in the skies, but through the windows of the eyes of your fellowman. Doing things for others—helping, serving, working with God in His still continuing creation of the Universe—you'll find is heaven. Don't look for love—give it. And it will find you in return. Love is the catalyst of happiness.

"Don't look for God only in the manmade structures called churches, but in the God-made cathedrals of the mountains, on the altars of unfolding flowers, in the sanctuary of the delivery room of the human birth, and in the incense of kindness. Look for God in the music of children's laughter; in the chalice of sacrifice for others; in the hymns of brother encouraging brother; and in the sacred silence of your conscience, where God speaks when we truly pause to listen for Him.

"Well, Sons, I wrote that fifteen years ago. I would not improve upon, or change it, today. It is my philosophy of the Divine power which rules the universe. It has been my guide. May you find it helpful in your own lives. So—there remains little else to say, dear Sons, except God bless you and guide your steps as He has guided mine. For we cannot see the path ahead, only the light of our dreams above the clouds to draw us on.

"I once had a dream when I was your age. I wanted to be a pioneer. My father had been born in a prairie schooner crossing the plains of Texas, and my grandfather had homesteaded claims for all of his sons. So I dreamed of wresting a home from the wilderness and building a house, and there bringing a wife and raising a family. I only wanted the simple joys of shared work and love—and above all keeping close to nature, the hills, the fields and trees. Well, years passed, and the rush of the dawning atomic world almost robbed me of the serenity of the forest I had visualized in my youthful dream of a pioneer life.

"And then one day, recently, I had a flash of insight and I saw how complete had been God's answer to my dreams. For Ginny and I have really pioneered after all—not exactly as my forefathers had, but on a frontier nevertheless—the new, the vast, the most exciting frontier man has yet faced—the frontier of outer space. And with that thought the peace of the forest once more moved through my soul—for I came to realize I had indeed been walking in a forest these past many years—among trees from whose timbers a new world will be built—and you, dear Sons, you are my tall trees. God bless you Greg, David, Malcolm and Starr—we love you so dearly. And, as you go forward, walk tall dear sons, walk a mile high—you are my tall trees..."

Once I had completed recording those letters on tape, a sense of great relief settled over me. I bathed, had a quick breakfast and caught the train for New York. Naturally, having been up all night, I immediately fell asleep and didn't wake up till a fellow commuter shook my shoulder when the train pulled into Grand Central Station.

At the office I got through the morning's correspondence and implemented the day's work for my assistants. The day's routine kept me too busy too think of my own concerns until the lunch hour thinned the area of people. Opening my desk I took out powdered soup, added hot water from the office tap, then with a sandwich from my briefcase I settled back to munch, sip, think, and stare out the window at the ant-like traffic threading the bottom of the East 46th St. canyon some twenty-three floors below.

What to do next? If my dream warning was accurate I was to exit life's stage at any moment. But I had faced that situation so many times in combat that the thought had no terror for me. My only serious concern was for those who were dependent upon me, and for those I loved. In the conflict of battle the probable instrument of my departure would be rifle or shell fire.

But now, in this civilian struggle for existence, and being in generally good health, I presumed the Reaper would most likely arrive on the scene in some form of traffic accident—I would be watchful.

The return to their desks of my assistants interrupted my cogitations. What should I do to ensure the smooth continuation of these international editions which my work had brought to life in Asia, Mexico and Britain? Through the glass office partition I watched my capable assistant editor, Drummond, bent over the proofs on his desk. Like myself he, also, had been an infantry officer in World War II. He was experienced in the transfer of command that must rise above the chaos of battle casualties—he could carry on, I need have no fear. And Naomi, my uncommonly efficient secretary, would see that the others understood what I would have done. Of course there was that carefully prepared loose-leaf book which I had worked up, sometime back, for my "boss man" Len. It was a complete SOP for establishing and operating a *Guideposts International Edition.* Yes, everything was in order here, nothing else was really necessary, my work would go on uninterrupted. It was a good feeling, for the people in those far-flung countries were deriving great help from the *Guideposts* sharing.

Again I looked out of the window, this time above the street's canyoned walls of many-windowed buildings. The abominable smog, shouldering its way between innocent clouds, was effectively screening out the cheerful rays of the midday sun. That manmade smog, I thought, is not unlike our negative emotions which frequently block out contact with Divine energy—some would call it God's love.

Love—that was the one unresolved, the one yet untouched subject, pushed into the back of my mind as I prepared for this unforseen departure. What about my beloved Ginny? My thoughts enveloped the fond object of my affections. Yet, what to tell her that had not already been whispered between us many times before, as we faced the probability of final separation in those tense war years? For we had reached, then, a union of heart and mind, so sure, so tender, so compellingly sweet in its attraction between our two hearts that time and distance did not intrude, and, when apart, we walked together on a plane above the physical. The years since, blessed by the shared joy of our children's presence within the circle of that bond of love, had only increased the enchantment.

"So, what now, Lord? Do we go together?" I pushed the question out toward infinity, beyond the smog-bound sun.

"Is that what you want?" The Lord's answer was patient, kindly—though I sensed a note of challenge beneath it.

"It's not what I want, is it? Lord, you summoned me. The dream was clear. My time is up. Very well, I accept that. I've always known it was Your part to send us here, and to call us back at some indefinite hour. And it's our part to fill the time between with our best efforts to understand Your purpose for our sojourn on this planet, and then to add something of ourselves to the evolution we perceive taking place here. But I think I recognize what's involved in Your present challenge. If I take Ginny with me now, I'll be taking her from the boys, and they need her—at least for another five or six years. All right, I'll go alone—though it won't be easy, for either of us..."

My reverie was interrupted, at this point, as my secretary came in with a sheaf of freshly typed letters. I thanked her, picked up a pen and began signing. Once more the press of work responsibilities engulfed me and the fragmentary conversation with God receded onto the back burner of my consciousness, not to be resumed until the following day.

Having slept deep and dreamless, both on the train home from work and throughout the night on the farm, now I found myself wide awake this morning, my every sense sharply aware, as the commuter train once more hurtled me toward New York City. The lush green of the crowding shrubs and trees along the railroad right-of-way flashed by with a soothing effect on my spirits. I was alive and well, moving once more into a day of challenging work. This was the third day since the Lord had spoken in my dream, and I was still here. The Reaper had not come to lead me across the valley of shadows...

"What happened, Lord?" I asked as my eyes brushed the countryside flashing by the train window and my soul responded to the beauty of this work of the Master.

"Weren't You there in my dream? Or did I only imagine it?"

"Yes, I was there, my son."

"Then why am I still here? What changed the plan?"

"You did, yourself, my son. You did something that was not anticipated. That is one of the least understood results of the law of free will by which I have given man the power to move this planet forward. Unforeseen consequences can be generated when man adds his own decision to any precise moment of unfolding events."

"And what, Lord, did I do?"

"You touched one of the secrets of the universe. You gave

advice to your sons against a background of music—a most unusual combination. Someday, not right away perhaps, but someday, you'll understand."
"Then what should I do now, Lord?"
"Just go on living as you were, my son, I'll not call you again before you reach the age of..." (here the Lord enjoined me not to disclose that time to anyone, saying...) *"I'll be watching how you fill the days till then."*

And so life has flowed on, for many years. But things have never been quite the same, as anyone who has experienced a brush with death will agree. Your sense of awareness is heightened, consideration for others deepened, and a keener edge tinges your spiritual hunger. Many of my comrades in combat have expressed like feelings. Some of us have felt that, since we were spared, we now have to live life with a double purpose—once each for ourselves and once to fulfill the unfinished lives of our comrades who did not return.

That weekend in New Bedford I did not explain my dream to Ginny, I simply played the tape for her. She agreed it was a timely summation of our thinking, and as each son left for college we gave him a copy of the tape to carry with him. But it was not until many years later, however, that I came to understand the significance of what God had meant about recording our advice to the boys against music. I discovered it in an unusual way...

In the spring of 1977, my brother Ted, then in his sixties, and for thirty years the owner-manager of Boston's classical music radio station, was assuming the additional profession of a clergyman. For his ordination ceremony as a Unitarian minister, he asked me to give a short address. I was reluctant to take part, feeling inadequate to add anything of fresh value to the ceremony. But, just three days before the ceremonies were scheduled to take place, I came across, quite by accident, an essay which fitted the occasion so uniquely that I called Ted and told him I would come to Boston and speak if he would let me read a brief paper. He agreed.

It rained heavily that Sunday, actually a torrential downpour. I was sorry for brother Ted, feeling it would reduce the number of people who might attend this, for him, all-important milestone event. Ginny and I arrived at the First Parish Church in Waltham in a veritable cloudburst. To our surprise the church was packed, with people standing in the aisles along the sides and at the back.

When it came my turn to speak I told the congregation that I had been sorting though a trunk full of old family keepsakes when I came across a small booklet titled "The Music of God." It was a brief essay, written in 1916 by the Rev. John Williams Jones, our own dear father. Dad was a clergyman whose perceptions were far ahead of his times. Let me share with you some of the insight which inspired him in that day—three score years ago—before the dawn of the atomic age:

"Among all the arts," he wrote, "music alone can be equally the language of civilization and spiritual humanity. Throughout all the ages of man, religion has allied itself with music, and man's intercourse with God has been aided and uplifted by concourse of sweet sound. The morning stars sang together, said the ancient seer, thus the inner and the outer world join together in divine harmony—The Music of God."

Then, here, Dad relates a summary of proven knowledge, so mighty in its implications that it majestically interprets the scientific reality of God. He writes:

"Nature is more full of music than we imagine. It has remained for modern science to develop this truth with startling vividness. All music is motion, and underlying all motion is the law of vibration. That which we call matter trembles—and its tremors go forth in waves of vibrations which have been estimated with scientific precision that staggers our imagination and stimulates our faith. Sound is that series of motion waves which begins at 16 vibrations per second, and goes to 36,500 per second. Musical sound, as we know it—being those vibrations from the lowest bass note of the great pipe organ, which sends out 16 waves of sound for every tick of the watch, up to the highest note of the piccolo which vibrates over 4,000 times per second."

At this point Dad's summary of statistical facts challenges our minds to follow his reasoning as he continues:

"The space between that and the next series of vibrations we know, is lost to our senses. At 100 million vibrations per second we have electricity, as it flows unseen and unheard along its visible and invisible channels. At 134,000 million vibrations per second we have dark heat, which may be felt but not seen—as it radiates and warms our physical being. At 483,000 million vibrations per second heat breaks into light and we can see the dark red of its glow—the first color of the rainbow prism. Then comes orange, then yellow, then green, then blue, then indigo, and lastly violet bursts forth into being at 708,000 million vibrations per second."

Now some of us may have read a part of these amazing statistics in our science classes, been momentarily awed, then shrugged and forgotten them. But this man, my father, was also a philosopher, who could not push aside bare facts without giving them the wings of imagination. So he concluded his essay, writing these words:

"And now we get a new vision of the poetry of nature. Light really sings. The sunshine is music...Thus is all nature like a great orchestra (or a grand organ) giving forth vibrations in different notes and chords of color...For each gorgeous cloud effect, every grouping of the stars, and all the radiations of countless suns are as choral anthems in God's ears. (And they would be so in ours if our ears were only delicate enough.)

"There is a melody and harmony of life in all its forms. From the tiniest protoplasm to the wondrous being of man, from the sensitive cell of the sea-urchin up to the human heart and soul and spirit. All is making music. And every throb of the pulse, every expansion of a cell, every thrill of a nerve with vital force, every bending of a muscle with vital power, has its part in the great hymn which all life is singing to the God who made it, from Whom it comes, and in Whom all life lives and moves and has its being..."

"All this vast universe of matter, pulsing with the power of hidden electricity, vibrating with the force of unseen heat, radiating with the glow of immeasurable light and breaking forth here and there with the glory of grand, beauteous color—all the universe is a voice and a song, so that the 'Music of the spheres' is indeed and truly 'music of God.'"

Looking out at the faces of the congregation as I read those lines, I was at the same time acutely conscious of the rhythm of the rainfall outside, and my mind flashed back to the moment I had talked with God about my taped letter to our sons. Now I knew, at last, what God had meant about music touching on secrets of the universe.

Now I knew for a certainty that each person's life is part of an unfinished symphony—the whole a never-ending score, a blending of harmonies, solo melodies and antiphonal passages vibrating with rapture in the amphitheater of God's ever-evolving universe. And, just as surely, every individual human life will contribute its note. With some it may be a solo stanza, with others only a breathless hesitation that provides accent, and with many it will be a succession of harmonic expressions, blending with the contributions of others, to create a melodic phrase of exquisite beauty.

I resumed my seat in the congregation, my mind in a whirl. Like a multicolored kaleidoscope design, the many spiritual revelations of my life were fitting themselves into a pattern that resolved previous conflicts and blended pragmatic realities with ethereal discoveries.

Now I was convinced that the sum total of my long, often capricious confrontations with God, when placed in ordered perspective, formed, of themselves, a musical composition. And my insistence upon logic as the language of believablity had woven my discoveries into a song that revealed new secrets of this eternally evolving Eden.

CHAPTER VI

My Non-retirement Years:

The Secret of God's Garden

𝕿 he final orchestration had really begun in the year of our nation's bicentennial. I had reached the age of seventy and it was time to retire from *Guideposts*. After 25 years as editor and creator of our overseas editions, it was appropriate that I pass the work to younger hands and move on to another career. In overlapping segments of my life, I had been successively: preacher's kid; actor-playwright-producer; combat soldier and active reserve officer; farmer and editor. Now, with the challenges of retirement facing me, I searched expectantly on the horizons of my life for signs pointing to the arena where I would find my next career venture.

At my retirement dinner, held in a New York City Chinese restaurant, (because half of our international editions were in the Orient) the dessert was, of course, Chinese fortune cookies. As I cracked the familiar cookie shell the little slip of paper which fell out onto my plate startled me with a message so surprising that I was sure my colleagues had inserted it purposely. But they insisted it was purely a coincidence; they had had

225

absolutely no part in its writing. The wordage on that bit of paper read: "Don't let a guidepost become a hitching post."

Well, I had certainly no intention of tying down to any state of mental or physical inactivity. Golf, fishing or casual beach lounging had no appeal for me. I craved action and mental involvement. By now our four sons had completed college and were out in the real world creating families and careers of their own. Ginny and I had only ourselves to think about, which meant freedom and a wide latitude for almost any activity we might undertake. A close friend had earlier invited me to run for Congress on the Conservative Party ticket. I had always been intrigued with the possibilities for social improvement involved in politics. Certainly there was both spiritual and physical challenge in such a career. Was now the time to enter this roiling water?

But our attention was also pointed in another direction—overseas. Husband and wife teams were being sought by the Executive Search program for volunteer service to aid business and industry in developing countries. In such work a retiree could pass on a lifetime of experience and acquired knowledge to help less fortunate people meet the technological challenge of this fast moving space age. On my last trip to the Orient for *Guideposts,* Ginny and I had met one such couple—a retired steel company executive from Indiana who, with his wife, was completing a two-year assignment as advisor to a Korean steel company in Pusan. The couple were enthusiastic over the work. "My expertise is genuinely appreciated by the Korean steel workers," said the American, "and my initiative is constantly being spurred by the intensity with which these Koreans tackle their jobs." The Indiana couple were planning to sign on for an additional two years.

The opportunities of such a retirement career intrigued us very much. From my own field of experience I could surely offer help in publishing, communications, leadership training, agriculture or even theatre arts. Was this the direction toward which to bend my efforts?

That winter I continued rising each day before dawn, even after retirement. For so many years I had watched the sun come up that now, even with no need to rush for the commuter train, I was reluctant to give up those moments of pure inspiration which came as I watched the sun's rays piercing the treetops along the ridge or glancing off the barn roof.

One morning in March I took my mug of coffee and went out into our small greenhouse, just off the kitchen, the better to watch the sunrise through the unobstructed glass walls. The sun was still at its southernmost swing of the season's pendulum, so as it rose slowly above the eastern hills its rays speared through the twisted branches of a giant willow. There had been a light rain during the night coating the trees, and the snow beneath them, with ice. Now the sun's rays turned the whole landscape into a fairyland of a hundred thousand small mirrors. Holding my coffee mug in both hands I sipped slowly, watching in fascination as the sun's light climbed through the glittering branches, until it surmounted the last gnarled limb to claim the sky as its own for that short winter day. I raised my coffee mug toward the bright sky—as our son Malcolm had done so long ago:

"Your health, God," I said softly. "Yes, this is indeed the day which You have made, and I am thankful to be alive in it. I understand fully, now, one of the immutable and least comprehended laws of Your ongoing universe—yes, through the centuries, from the beginning of time until this moment, this day never happened before in all of eternity. Today, on this planet, with all of its people forever changing as they react to events and the behavior of other persons, no individual is the same, now, as he was yesterday or ever will be again. Thus each new day, through our individual decisions, we are, every moment, creating something that never existed before. What a magnificent opportunity this day presents! God, while You are eternally creating changes in all of nature and the starry vault of heaven, You combine these with our individual efforts, as they touch the lives of other human beings, so that together we are continuing the evolution of the universe, are we not? And that's why You gave us free will, isn't it?"

"You, are thinking deeply, my son. But why do you suppose..." Here the Lord questioned gently, *"Why do you suppose so few people seem able to comprehend that?"*

"Because," I replied with some asperity, "we have had it dinned into us that we are miserable sinners, unable to accomplish anything on our own."

"You don't think you are a sinner?" The Lord's question was abrupt.

"Not born so, no. Oh, I may fail miserably, at times, to do what I could, or should, for Your world. Yet each new day You provide me a fresh chance. And logic insists that You, God, would not handicap me with the burden of original sin without first giving me an opportunity to meet, creatively, the challenges You have placed before the human mind and body on this planet. The trouble is, as I see it, man's spiritual outlook has been divorced from personal accomplishment in this life. Our spiritual advisers have been too 'other world' oriented."

"And you disagree with that premise?"

"Of course, Lord. First things first. I'm here now. You placed me here. I think I should make every effort to seek out Your purpose for that. And then I will work at the task for as long as You allow me to remain here. It's that simple. How else would I prove myself worthy of Your next world challenges?"

Outside the greenhouse glass the early sunlight danced obliquely over the icy frosting on the white snow. There was no wind to stir the dark green of the spruce boughs. The world seemed momentarily stilled by the chill. Yet underneath the cold blanket, field mice were tunneling through brown grass in search of food; tree roots were feeding, ever so slowly, on the sluggish moisture being released by the earth's rising temperature. The sweet sap was moving up, unseen, through the inner bark layers of the sugar maples. Spring was mounting through earth, and I was feeling it too. Once more I raised my coffee mug toward the glittering landscape outside my greenhouse walls.

"Yes, Lord, thanks again for the opportunities this day will bring. I only hope they will help show me what I should be doing with my retirement days."

"Have you not found the answer yet?" The Lord's reply had a note of gentle rebuke in it, which I had come to recognize as His reminder that I had not done my homework thoroughly.

"But haven't I, Lord? I've prayed for guidance, You know that. I can't just relax, now, and do nothing. Time is too important to be accomplishing things. Yet if I'm to presume that neither politics nor a Peace Corps type job is where I should put my effort, what shall I do? Always in the past, Lord, You have nudged me, but I feel nothing now. Have I finished all I can do for this world of Yours?"

"That's not the way you reacted on the night I summoned"

you in your dream." The Lord's voice was patient. *"Remember what you told Me then?"*

"Yes, of course, Lord, I said I had not finished raising my sons, the job was incomplete."

"And have you no other unfinished work, now? You asked for a new challenge, new adventure. But are you ready to move on? When you're gone can others finish what you left?"

Once more the Lord had sent me back to square one. Yes, there were unfinished tasks, which probably no one else would ever complete. In the past several years I had begun work on a number of stage and screen plays. I had outlined a nonfiction book (a manual on leadership) and I had written more than half of a historical novel. But what with my full-time job as an editor, with helping Ginny raise our four sons, and with working almost single-handedly at building our house, there had never seemed enough hours to devote to free-lance writing. And so the scripts were incomplete—as was also our own house. Dear, patient, Ginny never reproaching me for the thirty years of inconvenience entailed. I shook my head, half in self-reproach for my procrastination, half in wonder that I had been so slow, now, to see the task still before me.

"All right, Lord," I said aloud to the glittering landscape, "I'll get on to those unfinished jobs right away. And thanks for opening my eyes."

I smiled to myself as I faced up to the reality that once more in my life I had come face-to-face with a job that placed my feet, reluctantly, under a desk. Well, so be it. I'd get those manuscripts done, and the house finished, too, in record time. Maybe the world would be better for the effort. My house certainly, for it is built of concrete and stonework. It should last for several hundred years. The manuscripts? Some of them too, for they express ideas that could motivate people. Well, I'd do the best I could with them. Perhaps, then, the Lord would let me go on to some new adventure. But for now I had my orders and I was determined to move forward.

In the next four years I found myself busier than I had ever been before retirement. All week long I wrote from dawn till midday, then busied myself with carpentry in the afternoon. Our cement block house underwent a metamorphosis. We refinished the entire interior. The flat concrete, tar-covered roof became a steep, overhanging, peaked roof that produced an attic and a charming Tyrolean, chalet-style balcony. On a visit home our youngest son, admiring the soft pile of the wall-to-wall rugs that now covered the asphalt-tile-over-concrete-floors, said, "Why didn't we have these while we were growing up?"

My writing took on a fresh momentum. In addition to working on the unfinished manuscripts I undertook a weekly radio commentary program for Charles River Broadcasting Company of Boston. Researching the subject matter, writing the commentary and recording it on tape, occupied a full day each week. The work presented a new challenge, for the commentaries were largely political and essentially offered a conservative viewpoint. The program was well-received. So, I am still at it, and at 6 p.m. every Tuesday, the airwaves over New England carry my challenge signoff: "...Here's something you can do about it."

While my mind was responding nimbly to the stimulus of the daily writing regimen, a part of my anatomical apparatus was rebelling vigorously as I went about the task of remodeling our house. A combat injury to my legs had allowed arthritis, over the years, to gradually destroy the cartilage in the knees. Now, each day, I had increasing difficulty moving about, getting up and down, and the pain made it ever more difficult to complete my carpentry jobs. The net result was that in June of 1980, I ended up at Walter Reed Army Hospital in Washington, D.C. to undergo successive bouts of surgery.

It was during that ten-month hospitalization that my never-ceasing conversation with God uncovered a final, exciting challenge. Like the missing sheet in an orchestral composition it completed the melody of my life's spiritual seeking.

When I underwent the first surgery, on my left leg, the anesthesiologist used a spinal injection which numbed the lower half of my body but left me still conscious and able to converse with the doctors. That's just great, I thought, now I'll be able to see the whole operation and ask questions about the procedure.

I glanced down over the hospital sheet that covered me from neck to thighs. The surgeons and nurses (there must have been seven or eight of them) were all equally unidentifiable in face masks and formless headgear. I felt as if I were part of the cast in a segment of a M*A*S*H television show. With only their eyes showing it was not easy to tell who was who. One of the doctors I knew was my surgeon, the highly skilled Colonel David Tremaine, head of the Total Joint

Replacement Department of the Orthopedic Clinic. Tremaine was a deeply compassionate man with a gentle sense of humor. He reminded me of the character created by Alan Alda in M*A*S*H. Spotting his friendly eyes, now, as he completed preparations, I spoke up and started to raise my head.

"Hi, Doc. This is going to be fun. I didn't realize before I'd have a chance to watch you work."

The anesthetist, from his position above my head, pressed my shoulders down gently. I saw Doc Tremaine's eyes twinkle as he nodded to me, and then to someone I could not see. Immediately a pair of hands hung a towel over a metal bar that was a few inches above my chest and my view was cut off.

"Aw, Doc. that's not fair!" I protested.

"Can't give away all our secrets, now can we?" Tremaine's voice came from behind the towel, and I knew he was smiling at me under his mask.

"All right," I replied. "If that's the way it has to be then I'm going to sleep."

I looked up at the anesthetist, whose hands were still on my shoulders, and I winked acquiescence to his concerned care. Then I closed my eyes and, with the help of the sedatives already given to me, I was soon unconscious of what was going on in the busy operating room.

But I was not asleep, for I was somewhere else in the hospital, following a rolling stretcher on which was a covered figure whose face I could not see. The stretcher was pushed through a door. I followed, to find myself in an improvised operating room under a canvas roof. The masked medical attendants, working intently over a figure on the operating table, radiated an aura of peaceful calm. I could not hear what was being said, but the principal figure, who seemed to be giving instructions, was vaguely familiar. He turned in my direction, looking me straight in the eyes. His own eyes were kindly and filled with a depth of compassion that caused my whole body to tingle—and I knew that I was once more in the presence of God.

> "Well, Lord," I said, "here we are again. You, with this man, stretching forth Your hand, through his, to do what can be done with this moment of eternity. Somehow they have learned Your law of perpetual evolution, he and his team, so they're expending their utmost effort to do it as well as they possibly can—and this world will be better for what they do. That's the secret of accomplishing your purpose on this earth, isn't it? Taking whatever life puts before us, here and now, and turning it into something better because we touched it?"

The eyes in the masked face before me twinkled. Then he turned and held out his hand to the nurse who placed a bright instrument into the gloved palm.

"Scalpel, Dr. Pierce," she said. Instantly I knew why the figure had been so familiar—of course, it was Hawkeye, and I was watching a replay of M*A*S*H 4077! Or was it a replay? Or was I participating in a flashback to the reality of life on which that moving television series has so effectively been founded? The figure I now recognized as the formidable Hawkeye raised his head again in my direction and his eyes locked with mine. Once more the emotion of a compassion, so deep that it rocked my physically, looked out at me:

"Yes, Lord, I understand," I replied to the questioning eyes. "The real M*A*S*H personnel applied their compassion directly, one on one, to the soldiers' need. While their television counterparts were able, with their skills and dedication, to arouse a corresponding compassion in us, the multitudes of TV viewers, and we would become more sensitive persons because of it. Thus the personnel of both the real and the imaginary M*A*S*H units have left the world better for what they did with the moment before them."

I looked around the rugged operating room, then up, again, at the canvas roof—but it was gone. Now I was walking in the enclosed garden of the hospital, a unique architectural creation beginning on the third floor and extending upward to the sky. The garden is surrounded on all four sides by the glass walls of the patient's rooms, certainly one of the most effective applications of psychological architecture to patient's health. I had strolled briefly through the garden, with its three-story-high trees, the day before my scheduled surgery. Now I was back in the garden, but it wasn't quite the same. The concrete seating blocks had become outcroppings of rock, the trees were tall organ-pipe cactus, and the walls pushed themselves back until they were lost on a desert horizon. I started walking down a road that kept losing itself between hills covered with a riot of wildflowers so exquisite that at one place the scene made me wince with pain. I paused, eased myself down on a rock and reached out toward one of the delicate blossoms...

"Careful, don't move now; we're almost finished."

It was Doc Tremaine's voice. I opened my eyes. The towel had been removed from above my chest and I could see they were wrapping my whole leg, from hip to toe, in plaster. Two metal rods stuck through, on each side, below the knee. Just then one of the doctors picked up a large shiny instrument that looked like a pair of pruning shears. Quickly he cut the projecting metal rods back to less than a half inch from the plaster. I winced, for the medication was wearing off. I'd been on the operating table for over two hours.

Sometime later, back in the recovery room, I started to feel the pain. It was the beginning of an intense association with one of the most difficult of life's challenges. Physical pain is nature's way of telling us that something is out of order in our bodies. That is readily understood, though some of us wish nature didn't tell it quite so loud. I found night the most difficult time to wrestle with pain, especially when lights are out and you cannot read, write, or distract yourself with TV Some people I know find relief from pain by making intercessory prayers for others. This I have used frequently. But I have one other method I find helpful, either by itself or in conjunction with prayer. I explore with my mind the various ways in which people I know are doing things with their lives which seem to me to make the world better. Then I talk to God about them.

Some people will be doing big, exciting things. Others, the large majority of them, are doing things that almost no one is aware of, yet the world is better for that momentary brush of their lives in passing. Many people know about the work of Mother Theresa among the indigent and dying on the streets of India. But few know about the work of my friend Bruce Olson who is

bringing jungle Indians, the Motilone tribes of Columbia, into the mainstream of South American civilization, or my Korean friend Dr. Timothy Rhee's hospital
for the isolated fishermen on the island of Ulun-do in
the Japan Sea.

Yet, for every one such worker of modern miracles
there are hundreds of more, averagely inclined, individuals whose daily activities move this world forward.
In my own home area of Dutchess County in southern
New York, I number them by the dozens: Dr.
Genovese, our family physician who, long after all
other doctors had given up making maternity house
calls, found no hour too late or distance too great to
open the door of life; at our elementary school, two
teachers, Helen in third and Mary in fifth grade, so
inspired our sons that they finished classes far ahead
of their contemporaries; our plumber, Frank, a lover of
field and stream who plies his less-than-pleasant trade
with such pride in quality workmanship, that his installations will probably outlast the buildings in which he
places them; our young local Scout executive, Ron,
whose dynamic leadership had stoked the fires of ambition in our sons.

So I go on and on. The longer the pain lasts the more
I discover to talk about with God on worth and purpose
in the lives of my fellow man—and in so doing I find
my own life inspired anew by the way they have lived.

And I cannot leave the subject of physical pain without noting the frequently voiced questions: Why me?
or, Why does a God of love allow physical suffering?

From my own discoveries, in long debate with God, I arrived at this answer:

> "Our planet earth is a Divine workshop. We are here for the purpose of advancing God's continuing creation of the Universe, and we do that as each individual life adds ever new elements to it. But we must remember, as we watch birth going on around us, that pain is a part of the creation process."

It is this continuing creation process which so fascinates and inspires me, and draws me on to tilt with God about it. Towards the end of my stay at Walter Reed I resumed the sparring. The heavy plaster casts which I'd worn, first on the one leg then on the other, had now come off and physical therapy permitted exercise in the hospital's indoor pool.

The place was frequently empty as I slipped into the deep end, swam slowly to the center, dropped my feet down to reach the up-sloping bottom, then walked on, rising from heel to toe with each step, forcing maximum effort into the leg muscles—touch the end of the pool, turn around, repeat—back and forth across the water. One afternoon a brilliant, late sun came in through the high windows making the small waves of my progress throw dancing beams on the ceiling.

> "See that, Lord," I said half aloud as I moved through the water, "an appropriate commentary on life—back and forth, each day repeating what seems routine—our home life in the shallow waters, working world in the deep—back and forth, back and forth, yet each time strengthening needed faculties within us, creating self-confidence and courage to tackle new tasks never attempted before. And in the effort we toss shafts of light against the heavens."

I turned over and swam for a while on my back, watching the dancing reflections on the ceiling of the pool. They were like my thoughts, never still, yet full of bright hopes—suddenly a new thought intruded—suppose, suppose I should transpose that power into a formula?

> *"And why do you hesitate, my son?"* The Lord picked up my half-formed plan.
> "But should I undertake yet another piece of writing, Lord? I've still not finished those manuscripts you challenge me to complete. Would I be attempting too much?"
> *"Has any man ever used his full potential?"* God's voice vibrated through me as though I were a harp and He had lightly touched the taut strings. *"Has any man ever yet been able to measure the full capacity of the human brain?"*

I reached the end of the pool, pulled myself out and sat on the edge of the tile, my feet still touching the water. Gradually the wavelets quieted and the reflected lights ceased chasing themselves across the top of the room. But my thoughts did not match the calm of the empty swimming pool. Indeed they were racing round in my skull, knocking on my forehead, demanding to be let out, begging me to test them. A while back, my wife had suggested that I should put into writing the essence of my lifelong search for spiritual meaning:

> "Collect all those thoughts about God, which you've been discussing with me through the years," Ginny had said. "Put them into an essay, or theme paper. Do it for our sons if nothing else. You've never told them about your conversations with God."

These days in the hospital her words had returned to excite my imagination. I had even gone so far as to draw up an outline, and today I toyed with the idea of working it up into a book. Now the Lord had challenged me to step out on the project...

"All right, Lord, I'll do it. But I'll need You over my shoulder. I can't put it all down without seeming to contradict, or cross up other peoples beliefs, which are as valid for them as mine are for myself."

"Just put it down honestly, my son. Have you forgotten what you learned with Guideposts? *Don't try to destroy the spiritual security of others. Don't preach, just share."*

"Thanks, Lord, I'll be careful. I remember Mahatma Gandhi once said, 'I am Moslem, Hindu, Christian, Buddhist—I believe in God.' Most certainly that wise and gentle man had a rare ability to recognize Your image whether as the one God of Jew and Moslem, the three-in-one God of Christianity, the impersonal indwelling Force of Buddhism or the multi-faced God of the Hindu. Gandhi recognized You in everything. I wonder, could all mankind ever reach that same high level of comprehension?"

"Only if they wish it, individually. But a universal religious viewpoint is not necessarily a requirement for moving the planet forward, my son. Variety of viewpoint is part of the built-in challenge that creates evolution. What is needed most is tolerance, and a seeking to understand opposing religious views."

"But if some people have no religious convictions, like atheists or Marxists ?"

"Those, also, are a form of religious belief, my son. You have already learned that all mankind is created with a spiritual hunger. Communism, in spite of its disbelief in the supernatural Source of Creation, is actually a religion, because in dictionary terms religion is: 'a cause, principle or system of beliefs held to with ardor and faith,' and in Marxist theology the Supreme Source of Creation is man, not God. Because of this his basic spiritual hunger feeds on himself, and it is this spiritual cannibalism which threatens his own existence as

much as he threatens society itself."

"Then in that same vein, Lord, you're telling me that the atheist's disbelief in the Divine Creation is an extrapolation backward, a running from spiritual hunger, which in time becomes a religion of intense spiritual starvation?"

The thought of starvation, in any form, started my gastric juices to flowing. I looked at the clock at the far end of the pool and saw it was almost time for supper. My Ginny would be waiting patiently in the hospital parking lot. I moved to stand up, then paused, and on impulse raised one foot over the water, brought it down quickly to make a sharp splash. Once more, a legion of sun-kissed wavelets were racing across the pool, bouncing their diamond faceted reflections from walls and ceiling. It was a reassuring symbol—man has only to make himself move and the resulting vibrations are touched by God with light.

Within a few days I'd drawn up a finished outline for this book and sent it to a publisher for consideration. For better or worse, I was embarked on the difficult challenge to chronicle a lifetime of my conversations with God.

Thanks to the skill of the Army doctors and the careful nursing of the men and women on the staff of Walter Reed hospital I was given, quite literally, a new lease on life. Now, moving into the summer of 1981, with renewed enthusiasm I set about pursuing those unfinished tasks which had become my retirement career.

In February of 1982, we drove down in to Mexico to do research on one of the unfinished manuscripts. In this case it was a play I had wanted to write concerning events which had occurred during the turbulent years of the Mexican Revolution, from 1857 to 1917. The story of the play, a creation of fiction based on historical facts, has to do with the most violent period in the struggle between the state and the power of the Roman Catholic Church.

We returned to Los Angeles in May, with voluminous notes and an outline that, within a year, became the finished manuscript of my play.

But it was on that return trip from Mexico to California (in May of 1982) that I had a series of discussions with God which captured the celestial vista which I'm now putting down on these final pages of my spiritual chronicle.

Ginny and I were driving through the desert country of southern Arizona. At sundown we changed places and I took over the wheel. Twilight is short in the desert so, even though we were heading west, the magic of those Arizona sunset clouds held the sky in breathtaking splendor for only fleeting moments. Then the night sky took over, a hundred thousand stars hung out their ancient patterns against the velvet depth of infinity. Like a sleepy child closing its eyes, the red-gold slit of sky on the horizon blinked shut, and on the near-deserted highway I was driving into the starlit bowl of eternity.

I glanced over at Ginny. Her head was nesting in a pillow against the window, her eyes closed. I reached over to brush her cheek lightly with my fingers, then turned my attention again to the shadowy stretch beyond the reach of the car's headlights. How many years ago was it that we had traveled over this same desert, in the opposite direction, heading for our "wedding night" in a Phoenix hotel? Counting with my fingers on the steering wheel I ticked off thirty-eight—almost four decades—a lifetime of experiences: wars, children and changing careers that challenged every fiber of our joint capacities. I raised my eyes to the distant horizon:

"Thank You, Lord. They've been good years, wonderful years. How little did I imagine what life had in store for me that night I camped in the high peaks above the Yosemite. I remember how bright the stars shone that night. Look at them now, out there above this Arizona desert. The atmosphere is so clear I must be seeing twice as many. Yet they are the same whether I could see them or not."

"No, not quite the same, my son. In the years since that night each star is brighter, or dimmer, because evolution never stops. Stars, planets or human beings, they are forever changing."

"Then, in the evolution of human beings, is the Darwinian theory correct? Did man evolve from the ooze of primordial slime as Professor Darwin would have us believe?"

"Does it seem logical, my son?"

"No, Lord. I find it totally unreasonable to believe that the intricate composition of the human body and spirit is the result of chance selectivity as survival of the fittest. The bare statistics of a few ancient skulls or bones does not convince me. There are too many gaps in Darwin's hypothesis."

"Then you would prefer the Biblical theory of man's creation?"

"No, Lord, not that either. It is too simplistic."

"You don't think that I could create man from dust?"

"Oh, yes, I do. But I don't think You did it from the dust of this earth. That was only the view of ancient sages who, several thousand years ago, tried to account for man, and our galaxy of planets, as they viewed the possibilities from their available knowledge at that point in time."

"And how do you view it, my son, from your point in time?"

"I know, Lord, that our planet is but one celestial body in Your universe of billions and billions of stars, planets, and galaxies, forever in evolution. I believe You, Lord, have created us with eternal curiosity to delve into, and uncover the secrets of that universe and, with our free will, to take part in its perpetual evolution. I believe we came here from elsewhere in the universe, and that we will move on beyond this life, to continue the evolution of other planets."

"And how did you reach that psycho-anthropological outlook, my son? You realize, don't you, that it contradicts much current religious thought?"

"I only express what seems logical to me, Lord. Others need not think as I do. But neither can I do less than believe what reasoning man, in this 20th century, is discovering about our earth and its place in Your expanding universe."

"But if the religions of your world do not agree with you, my son? Is there no wisdom in their teaching?"

"Certainly, Lord, they do a great deal to satisfy man's spiritual hunger. They have, each in their own way, pointed to You as the Source of Creation. But they still cannot account for the process of that creation, Your purpose for mankind in its evolution, or give a logical rationale for the future use of our unique, individual personalities after this period of growth is completed here on earth."

"Is not the Bible sufficiently clear on that, my son?"

"No, Lord, and You know it. As a record of man's spiritual seeking it is inspiring and beautiful reading. But as an interpretation of Your purpose and the evolution of Your universe it is inadequate, because the record stopped long, long ago.

"And just what, my son, do you think needs to be done?"

"Why should You not, God, give new revelations to us here, now, in this last quarter of the 20th century? The scope of our understanding, today, is as vastly different from the days in which Holy Scriptures were written as an atomic rocket is from a donkey cart. Is it not possible, situated as we are on the technological edge of an electronically-controlled space age, that You, God, might now reveal Yourself, and Your purpose for our existence, in a manner equally beyond the concepts of mankind living in those days so many thousands of years ago?"

"Yet isn't that taking place right now, my son? Many others, like yourself, are seeking new answers—and finding them. But

the sum of their discoveries becomes visible to the many only when perceived by individuals who bring them to the attention of others. As you have learned, my son, the skies will not open with a celestial declaration. Man himself must pry it open. It is the responsibility I gave to him with the gift of free will."

Again, as throughout the years of our discourse, the Lord was holding out to me the Divine Gauntlet. If I wanted 20th century revelations I must look for them in the marketplace of today's living—and, when found, share them.

The car sped on through the night. Above the ribbon of concrete, on which our vehicle rolled swiftly towards our next day's encounter with destiny, the arc of the heavens sparkled with light from uncounted billions of stars. Much of that heavenly light, so modern astronomers have discovered, began moving toward planet earth eons of light-years before this moment—truly a mind-expanding concept. Tomorrow, I decided, when we get to Tucson, I will go out to the Kitt Peak National Observatory and begin searching among their recorded discoveries for connections between scientific findings and spiritual truths.

But, as so often happens in life, my good intentions for the next day were sidetracked and I never got out to Kitt Peak. It is only now as I conclude this book, that my thoughts have returned to the discourse of that night. So, I cast about for ways to illustrate the spiritual insights of modern astronomy and found, to my great surprise, that I had on the bookshelf of my den-library a ready-made summary of the subject in the November 1973 edition of *Arizona Highways*. The entire issue of that beautiful magazine was devoted to cosmology and

astronomy. In the introduction editor Joseph Stacey
says:

"...the cosmic view includes a broad horizon from the tiniest
particle of the atom to the incredible vastness of space... The
origin and development of life in the Universe begins with the
atom. Whatever the plan and design for the uses of the mi-
raculous particle, man is the reference point... In one generation man can see only so far. With succeeding generations he
sees farther all the time."

And, setting tones for the colloquium was a quote
from Albert Einstein, who said, in part:
"The most beautiful and most profound emotion we
can experience is the sensation of the mystical. It is the
sower of all true science...this knowledge, this feeling
is at the center of true religiousness."
Articles in the magazine covered the work of some
of the world's most outstanding astronomy observato-
ries, four of which are located within a fifty mile radius
of Tucson: Kitt Peak National Observatory; University
of Arizona's Steward Observatory; The Smithsonian
Astrophysical Observatory; and the National Radio Astronomy Observatory. Their facilities include 25 of the
world's largest, most advanced telescopes, devoting full
time to research. In the work of these dedicated men
and women of science I found ready answers to what
the Lord surely meant when he told me that 20th century revelations were even now being made. Of special
interest to me was an actual photo of the night sky
above us revealing multi-millions of pinpoints of starlight, against which the editors had superimposed a

quotation from scientist-writer Harry Golden which said, in part:

> "I know that there are at least four billion suns in the Milky Way—which is only one galaxy...and vast millions of them have whole planetary systems...This is only our own small corner of the universe...How many galaxies are there? Billions...Within the range of our biggest telescopes there are at least one hundred million galaxies such as our own Milky Way, and that is not all, by any means. Scientists have found that the further you go into space with the telescopes the thicker the galaxies become...and there are billions of billions as yet uncovered to the scientist's camera and the astrophysicist's calculations."

The sum of those scientific statistics points up the inadequacy of Biblical religions' thinking which proposes a vague spiritual heaven somewhere in the sky, unrelated to the actual celestial bodies now known to occupy the infinity of outer space. Such religious theory, which sings about an eternity with God in which there will be no dawning and no sunset, ignores completely the factuality of God's magnificent, perpetually evolving, universe. I believe the answer to the next world's location shines at us each time we gaze into those pinpoints of starlight in the vault above.

Finally, on the concluding page, Mary Elizabeth Burke, in a hauntingly beautiful "Soliloquy While Watching A Sunset," tells us:

> "...In this perfectly beautiful setting, a Reasoning Power determined, 'Win or lose, I am going to introduce the element of free will into the thinking mechanism of man on this planet. What will he do with this irrevocable law (which is) forcing him to ultimately determine his own destiny? And yet, I will be

kind; I will establish universal truths...laws to assist in making his determination, in the process of his evolution.'"

So, once again, God had answered my seeking. Carefully I filed that issue of *Arizona Highways* for future reference. Most large libraries, I feel sure, will have it available for others to enjoy. But that was not the only printed record of modern revelations that I unearthed in my own library. There was also the copy of a book published by Souvenir Press of London in 1972, titled *"We Are Not The First: Riddles of Ancient Science."*

In this work, historian Andrew Tomas offers a collection of anthropological discoveries, ranging from ancient cave-wall drawings, to jungle covered earthworks, to artifacts from historical digs, arranged by the author to support his theory that intelligent human beings have, from time to time in millenniums past, suddenly appeared on planet earth. Tomas suggests they came from other worlds.

Thus do revelations come as I follow God's nudge to keep seeking. Some are more lucid than others, some carry within themselves the seed that spurs yet more search. Each day I find God's universe more exciting to explore; each day I am more appreciative of my chance to share in the development of His planet earth. For I know that everything I do here can make me more valuable to His continuing evolution in a next world to which He will call me. In the meantime I am eagerly following a clarion, eight-word challenge, which came to me, once, above the heads of a foreign multitude crowded into a great stone building in a place some six degrees below the equator, on the edge of the South China Sea.

I was in Djkarta, capital city of the Republic of Indonesia, that equatorial nation comprising some hundreds of islands in the South China and Java seas. That particular Sunday, in the fall of 1964, I went to attend early service at the Catholic cathedral. The courtyard of the church was crowded with people come to attend the 7:00 a.m. Mass. Seated just inside the iron gateway and along the side walls, were dozens of ragged women, children and old men. Some were lame, others showed a variety of physical handicaps, but all held out their hands for alms. Here was want and physical hunger, but few of the churchgoers stopped to give before going through the great doors.

Inside the huge church building I found every pew completely filled, while standees packed in the space between the last row of pews and the back wall. Here was spiritual hunger. I squeezed myself in, between warm bodies and the cool stones of the church wall. The familiar Latin service began. When it came time for the sermon, (the homily as it is called in the Roman communion) the priest came halfway down the church to a pulpit built against one of the immense granite pillars along the side aisle.

For his sermon the priest spoke in a native Indonesian tongue, a language I did not know, so of course I could not understand a word of what was said. But he had a strong voice and a pleasing personality so I listened, trying to guess from intonation and gestures, what his subject might be.

Suddenly three words in English burst out from the pulpit—"Time is money!" Instantly I was alert. But the priest resumed talking in his Indonesian tongue. Now why did he use that phrase in English? Undoubtedly because it was familiar to the populace, as are other bits of English which have become bywords around the world—like O.K., Hello, or Hot Mama.

The priest continued his sermon in Indonesian but soon, once again, the priest cried out, "Time is Money!" By now I was thoroughly aroused and watching intently the face and gestures of this energetic preacher in a strange pulpit in a foreign land. As he continued his spirited homily, in words I could not fathom, I decided I would have to see him afterward and have someone translate for me what the message was that could only be expressed in those three English words. Then, for the third time, the Anglican phrase rang out over the heads of the crowded congregation. "Time is money," the priest's voice rose triumphantly. "Time is money—with which we buy eternity!"

Ah, what a stirring challenge was put forth in that couplet of eight words. I have never forgotten it, for surely God spoke to me that day as never before. Time, here on earth, is for a mighty purpose—I must use it well.

So, now I come to a pause in this chronicle. It is not finished, for I will never cease to maintain dialogue with my Creator. But my pen has caught up with my wayward confrontations with God and I cannot put down what is yet to come—for neither God, nor myself, knows what will transpire when I meet and must make decisions, to resolve the continuing evolution of this fascinating planet.

As my pen hesitates above the paper, anxious to conclude these long months of earnest effort to translate intangible emotions into perceptible experiences, I push back from the desk and glance out my library window. A heavy fog is moving through the forest's edge on this north side of our farmhouse. The late October winds have completed disrobing the trees. Now, not unlike the naked men of our battalion as they executed that fantastic cootie-dance in the dockside warehouse just before we sailed for combat duty in France, the trees of my woodlot brigade sway gently, their bare limbs and upright bodies unashamedly accepting the sensual caress of a faceless, gypsy fog.

Most of our trees are young second-growth. But there are two great trunks, two hoary patriarchs on the edge of the woodlot—one a giant black oak, the other a sugar maple. Like a pair of gods they have guarded that corner of the forest since long before my generation came to this part of Quaker Hill. The oak had probably attained good size when Henry Hudson sailed the Half Moon up from New York Harbor, and within its rugged heart may be embedded rifle balls from George Washington's troops who were encamped in these stony hills before the general became our nation's first president.

In my own lifetime I have traveled far, on several occasions more than halfway around the world. But the oak tree waits, patiently, in one place. Yet, in God's good time, the world itself may come and pass by my oak tree. Even now oak branches brush my chimney and the television antenna firmly secured to its side. And who is to say that the fibers of the oak do not possess the transmitting power to tap the panorama of the world events which daily crowd those TV airwaves? The oak tree waits for evolution to come to it; mankind, inspired by a divinely implanted curiosity, goes forth to meet it.

My attention returns from the window to the unfinished manuscript on my desk. I pick up my pen and make this note, which I am to remember:

"Throughout all eternity, today, this moment never happened before.

God created me as a unique personality that has no duplicate in all of the universe.

I am given the privilege, if my free will accepts the challenge of the moment, to create, with God, something that never existed before—

The planet earth is God's workshop, where mankind, gifted with free will, creates his own destiny for worlds to come.

Time is money. I must use it well, for with it I am buying eternity."

Amen